TERRIFIC
Totes
&
Carryalls

TERRIFIC Totes & Carryalls

40 BAGS TO SEW FOR SHOPPING, WORKING, HIKING, BIKING, AND MORE

Carol Parks

Lark Books

Art and production: Celia Naranjo
Photography: Evan Bracken, Light Reflections
Illustrations: Bernadette Wolf
Editorial assistance: Valerie Anderson

Library of Congress Cataloging-in-Publication Data

Parks, Carol,
    Terrific totes & carryalls : 40 bags to sew for shopping, working,
hiking, biking, and more / Carol Parks.
        p. cm.
    Includes index.
    ISBN 1-57990-019-4
    1. Tote bags. 2. Sewing. I. Title.
  TT667.P38 1998   97-4653
  646.4'8—dc21   CIP

10 9 8 7 6 5 4 3 2 1

First Edition

Published by Lark Books
50 College Street
Asheville, North Carolina 28801, USA

©1998 Lark Books

Distributed by Random House, Inc., in the United States, Canada, the United Kingdom, Europe, and Asia
Distributed in Australia by Capricorn Link (Australia) Pty Ltd., P.O. Box 6651, Baulkham Hills Business Centre, NSW 2153
Distributed in New Zealand by Tandem Press Ltd., 2 Rugby Rd., Birkenhead, Auckland

Printed in Hong Kong by Oceanic Graphic Printing, Ltd.

ISBN 1-57990-019-4

Contents

Introduction

Totebags, carryalls, backpacks, and their kin are the working bags in our lives, essential companions on every kind of trip from the daily business commute to a well-planned annual vacation. It seems we no longer can leave the house without carrying something! Making bags like these is great fun for a number of reasons. For one thing, there is no limit to the design potential! A simple tote-bag is so quick to make that you can experiment with all sorts of stitching and decorative techniques without investing a great deal of time. But perhaps the best reason to make such bags is to get exactly the size and shape you need, with pockets that will exactly accommodate the gear you will put into them.

On the following pages are designs for bags of every shape and description, as well as plenty of ideas for special carriers to meet special requirements. Remember your friends and family members when you look at the photos—a new custom-made carryall is a thoughtful gift.

Fabric choices

Most carryalls, totes, and bags of this sort are intended to carry a good-sized load. If this is a consideration for your own project, look for medium to heavy firmly woven fabric with little or no stretch. Sturdy cotton, linen, and hemp—or blends of these—will work well for many of the models shown in this book, and in fact are the fabrics chosen by many of the designers. These fabrics are easy to sew and to press, and will wear quite well.

Stores that sell decorator fabrics usually have a good selection of slipcover-weight cottons and cotton blends, and these are especially suitable for totebags and carryalls. Often such fabrics are finished for soil and stain resistance, a plus where wearability is concerned. The finish will not withstand laundering or repeated dry cleaning.

Heavier decorator fabrics, such as upholstery materials, can be interesting for bags too. Beware of those that are coated on the wrong side; the slip-resistant coating causes stitching difficulties. If your heart is set on such a fabric, try using a coated needle or needle lubricant to prevent skipped stitches.

Fabrics made specifically for outdoor wear—Cordura and the like—produce exceptionally durable bags. These also may call for some adjustments in stitching techniques. Practice with a scrap to find the best stitch tension and length, and the best needle to use with the fabric.

Sewing with Leather and Suede

Leather is a traditional choice for working bags for several reasons. It is beautiful and durable, and with some maintenance will age gracefully and give years of service. Some leathers are even machine washable. Leather is not the least bit difficult to sew, and in fact is actually far easier to manage than many woven or knit fabrics. Follow the guidelines below and success

is almost guaranteed! If you have never worked with leather, a bag is a good beginning project.

• Choose leather designated as "garment weight" for use with a home sewing machine. Cut each piece separately rather than from doubled leather. If there are thin spots on the leather, plan so they aren't placed at areas of the bag that will be subjected to stress.

• Do not use pins; they will leave permanent marks. Use pattern weights for cutting, and use small binder clips or glue baste in the seam allowance to hold the pieces for stitching.

• Apply sew-in interfacing to prevent stretching in areas of stress. Use polyester or cotton-wrapped polyester thread.

• Use a machine needle designated for leather, the size appropriate to the thickness of the skin. For hand stitching, use a glover's needle.

• To reduce drag when stitching, use a Teflon-coated presser foot, or apply adhesive-backed Teflon to the bottom of a presser foot. A walking or even-feed foot also works well.

• Finger press seams open, then tap with a rawhide or wooden mallet to flatten them. Trim the seam allowances at an angle to bevel the edges. Topstitch seam allowances in place, or glue them with a permanent contact cement.

• Since leather and suede do not ravel, it is not necessary to overcast edges. Hems may be stitched, or can be glued with contact cement.

Linings

Many of the designs in this book call for lining. A lined bag not only looks better, but will wear longer. A lining also allows you to add interior pockets.

Look for lining fabric that is the same or lighter weight than the outer bag fabric, and one that is equally durable so that the lining won't wear out before the bag itself does. Light or brightly colored lining makes it easier to find things at the bottom of a large bag. To add an element of interest, try a contrasting lining—a cheerful print with a neutral exterior, or a complementary color or texture. Lining offers an opportunity to experiment with surface design, too. Try stenciling or painting designs on the fabric. Only you will see the results unless you choose to show your work.

Underlining and Interlining

An additional fabric layer sewn as one with the outer fabric or lining gives the bag a smoother appearance and helps pro-

tect the contents. Underlining, applied to the wrong side of the outer fabric, adds to the bag's durability. Interlining, sewn to the lining fabric, provides more padding.

Fusible or sew-in interfacing, in an appropriate weight for the fabric, gives the outer fabric more body. Light- to medium-weight batting is a good choice when extra thickness is desirable. It can be quilted to the outer fabric to add a design element besides.

Interlining helps strengthen the lining, a consideration if the lining fabric is light in weight and when pockets are added. Here, too, batting is a good choice for the extra thickness it contributes. Sew-in or fusible interfacing also can be used, as can almost any lightweight fabric.

Buttons and Buckles and Such

For working bags like backpacks and large totes, the findings should be strong and durable. There are a number of mail order suppliers that offer traditional handbag hardware and specialized fittings for backpacks, and many of them advertise in sewing magazines. Stores that sell outdoor equipment usually stock fittings for replacement and repair. Alterations shops and leather repair shops sometimes have a supply of buckles and fasteners. Some clever sewers we know buy bags and belts at thrift stores, cut off the interesting hardware and buckles, then throw away the rest.

Use your imagination, too! An interesting non-traditional closure can be the focal point of a bag, as many of our designers have shown.

Zippers, too, should be chosen for durability. Metal zippers, zippers intended for use on outdoor clothing, and "sports" zippers are better choices than the standard garment-weight variety for large bags. Upholstery shops often sell heavy-weight zippers by the inch, cut to order.

Preparing the Fabrics

In order for a bag to be washable, it is necessary to preshrink the fabrics before you cut. This simply means washing and drying the outer fabric and lining as you intend to wash the finished bag. Then press the material carefully, pressing in the direction of the lengthwise grain to avoid stretching the fabric. Fusible interfacing should be preshrunk according to the manufacturer's instructions.

Square the fabric before you cut so that the crossgrain threads are exactly perpendicular to the selvages. Washing the fabric to preshrink it usually will straighten the grain somewhat. You also can square the piece by pulling it diagonally, then steam pressing it to shape. To determine the straight crossgrain, clip into the selvage and pull a thread across the fabric. Cut along the mark left by the pulled thread.

Pockets

One of the greatest rewards of making a carryall or tote is that you can add all the pockets you need, inside and out, and adapt them exactly to suit you. The designers whose bags appear on the following pages offer dozens of pocket variations, so use their ideas to customize your own bag.

For many bag styles, it is easy to add a pocket across the outside simply by cutting a piece the width of the bag side but shorter in height, hemming the upper edge, then sewing it into the side and bottom seams. This pocket is used for the tote on page 11 and for several other designs. The same sort of pocket can be added to the lining too, as for the child's backpack on page 120.

A patch pocket is one of the quickest kinds to make, and can be used on the outside or inside of a bag. Attach the pockets to the bag or lining sections before assembling the bag.

For a basic patch pocket, cut a rectangle of fabric with seam allowance added to the sides and lower edges, and a hem allowance at the top. Hem the top first. Press under the seam allowances and topstitch the pocket in place with two rows of stitching.

If the pocket will be used to hold bulky items, add a pleat at the bottom for ease. Place the fabric over the actual item if possible to determine the amount of ease needed. To cut the fabric, add twice the pleat depth to the width of the piece. Fold a pleat at the lower edge before pressing under the seam allowance. A strip of elastic can be threaded through the hem to hold in the fullness at the top.

It is also possible to layer the patch pockets, smaller ones on the outside of larger ones. Sew the smaller ones in place before attaching the largest to the bag.

Subdivide a large patch pocket into compartments with lines of vertical stitching once the pocket is in place. If pleats are needed for ease, plan one for each compartment.

There are several ways to equip a pocket with a zipper. The easiest is to simply add a seam across the pocket fairly close to the top. Cut the fabric with seam allowance all the way around rather than with a hem allowance at the top. Remember to included seam allowance for the added seam. Install the zipper in the seam, then fold under the seam allowances around the edge and topstitch the pocket in place.

The pocket also can be made as a complete unit, then attached to the bag. Cut a piece of fabric twice the desired pocket length, plus seam allowance at each end. Baste the short ends together and install the zipper in the seam. Fold the resulting tube so that the zipper is at the front. Open the zipper and stitch the sides. Turn the pocket right side out and top-stitch in place.

Pockets with Flaps

The addition of a flap to a patch pocket makes the pocket more secure and offers an opportunity to display a one-of-a-kind button or interesting closure. You might also use a hook and loop tape closure or a snap.

Plan the finished flap to be ⅛ to ¼ inch (approximately .5 cm) wider than the finished pocket. Allow sufficient length so the flap won't look skimpy when it closes over a filled pocket.

Cut two pieces—one will be the lining—with seam allowance added on all sides. Round the two lower corners if you wish. With right sides together, stitch the pieces at the sides and across the lower edge. Trim, and turn right side out. Baste the raw edges together along the seamline. Topstitch the finished edges, if desired, and work a buttonhole if your design calls for one.

Chalk mark a placement line on the bag ½ to 1 inch (1.5 to 2.5 cm) above the pocket, allowing the greater distance for a larger pocket. Place the flap lining side up, raw edges toward the pocket and the basted seam on the placement line. Stitch along the basting, backstitching securely. Trim the seam allowance. Fold the flap downward, and press. Topstitch across, approximately ¼ inch (.5 cm) from the seam, enclosing the seam allowance.

The Sewing Machine

Since the fabrics used for totes and other such bags often are heavier than those used for garments, give your machine a little extra attention to ensure good results with your project. Clean it before your begin, and oil it if necessary.

You may need to use a larger needle than usual to accommodate thick fabric and seams. Some fabrics, particularly those intended for outdoor equipment, respond best to a coated needle with a sharp point. Leather calls for a special chisel-point needle. Whatever your fabric, if you encounter stitching difficulties, check with your machine dealer. Whenever a new fabric is introduced to the market there is soon a new machine needle to cope with it.

Presser feet, too, can make a difference when you sew with heavy or coated fabrics. A Teflon-coated foot will reduce drag with leather and coated fabrics. A walking foot or even-feed foot is helpful with stretchy or very coarse fabrics.

Sewing Techniques

The strength and durability of a carryall or backpack depend to a great extent upon the fabric from which it is made. Equally important is the way it is made. The use of interfacing, double-sewn seams, and topstitching all contribute toward making a bag that can bear up under years of tough treatment without coming apart at an inopportune moment.

Add interfacing to areas that are subject to stress or stretching, like the straps, around an upper edge hemline, and pockets. Use either fusible or sew-in, as firm a weight as will work with the fabric.

To reduce strain on the seams, use a seam that is stitched twice. French seams, flat-felled seams, and topstitched seam allowances all contribute to the strength of the bag.

• French seams are quite strong and, because they are finished on the wrong side, look neat when the bag is unlined. To sew a French seam, stitch the seam with fabric wrong sides together, using half the seam allowance. Trim away half the seam allowance and press the seam open. On the wrong side, crease along the seamline. Stitch again with right sides together, enclosing the seam allowances.

• Flat-felled seams can be sewn with either right sides together or wrong sides together. In the former case, the seam and one row of stitching will be visible on the right side of the bag. In the latter case, there will be two visible lines of stitching. This seam works best with fabric that is easy to crease and press.

Stitch the seam and press the seam allowances to one side. Trim away half the under seam allowance. Fold the upper seam allowance around and under the trimmed seam allowance; press. Stitch again close to the folded edge.

• Serged seams can be strengthened by pressing the seam allowances to one side then topstitching them in place. The same technique can be used for overcast seams sewn with a regular machine. Seam allowances also can be pressed open and topstitched in place to make them more durable.

• With bulky fabrics, trim and grade seam allowances to eliminate visible ridges on the bag exterior. Trim the seam allowances so that the one closest to the bag section is longer and the inner one shorter. If the fabric is not too thick, you can trim and grade both layers at the same time by holding the scissors at an angle as you cut.

• Stitch straps securely. If straps ends are incorporated into a seam, also stitch across them several times in the seam allowance. When they are sewn to the bag exterior, stitch around each end then reinforce by stitching an X across the end.

• Reinforce each upper corner of a patch pocket with a triangle or a bar tack. Use a bar tack, too, at each end of a zipper.

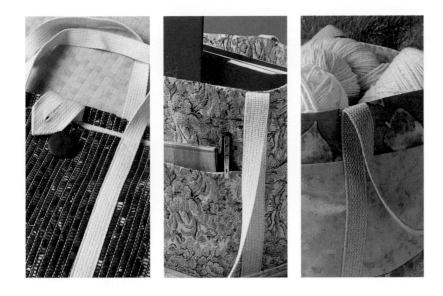

The Totebag Tradition

The familiar, friendly tote has served us well for generations, carrying every sort of thing from books to baby gear, picnics to tools of our trades. Most of us have a collection of them in every size and shape, souvenirs of vacation trips or decorated with store logos.

The style is a simple one to sew up. The bag can be lined or left unlined. It can be customized with pockets inside or out. It can be decorated in any way you wish. Fabric should be chosen with an eye for durability. If lighter weight fabric is used for the sides of the bag, you might use heavier material for the bottom section.

Purchased cotton, polyester, or nylon webbing 1 inch (2.5 cm) or more in width makes strong handles or shoulder straps. As an alternative, handles can be made from bag fabric itself and embellished with stitching as shown on the tote on page 16.

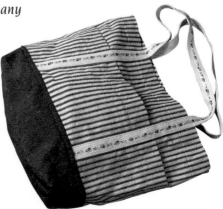

A traditional tote has hundreds of uses; this one was designed to keep the gardening tools together. To add an appropriate floral element, embroidered ribbon was stitched to the strap webbing before the straps were attached. **Design: Tracy Doyle**

A Basic Totebag

Pretty cotton in ticking stripes is teamed with natural cotton canvas to make a tote that is both sturdy and attractive. A pocket across one side is divided into thirds by the handle stitching. A second pocket could be added along the other side—just allow a little extra fabric. Our bag is not lined, but if you wish to line your own model, the instructions are given below.

The finished bag is 11½ inches (29 cm) wide, 12½ inches (31.5 cm) high, and 5½ inches (14 cm) deep.

SUPPLIES

- Fabric: 1 yard (.95 m) 54 to 60 inches (137 to 152 cm) wide, or 1⅜ yards (1.3 m) 45-inch (115-cm) fabric.
- For bag with contrast bottom: Main fabric, ½ yard (.5 m) 54 to 60 inches (137 to 152 cm) wide or 1 yard (.95 m) 45-inch (115-cm) fabric; for contrast bottom, ⅜ yard (.35 m) any width.
- Webbing: Polyester or cotton, 1 inch (2.5 cm) wide, 2⅞ yards (2.65 m) for shoulder straps, or 2 yards (1.85 m) for shorter carrying handles.

CUTTING

1. For the sides, cut two pieces 18 inches (46 cm) wide by 13 inches (33 cm) long.

2. For the bottom, cut one piece 18 inches (46 cm) wide by 12 inches (30.5 cm) long from the same or contrast fabric.

3. Cut one piece (or two) for the pocket, 18 inches (46 cm) wide and 9 inches (23 cm) long.

CONSTRUCTION

1. Hem one long edge of each side section and the pocket. Fold and press 2 inches (5 cm) to the wrong side. Fold under the raw edge ½ inch (1 cm) and press again. Stitch close to the fold.

2. Place the pocket, right side up, on the right side of one side section, aligning the ends and lower raw edges. Machine baste around the raw edges in the seam allowance.

3. To mark placement for the straps, fold the side sections in vertical thirds and press creases. Cut the webbing in two and position a length on each side section over the creases, aligning the ends with the side lower raw edge. Stitch close to each edge of the webbing. To reinforce at the top, stitch an X on each side of the strap in the hem area.

4. With right sides together and using ⅝ inch (1.5 cm) seam allowance, stitch the sides of the bag to the bottom. Overcast the seam allowances as one and press

Heavier weight fabric was used for the bottom to make the bag more durable.

Pretty cotton tapestry fabric, fairly heavy in weight, makes a tote that keeps up appearances and can carry a heavy load besides. Linen-textured cotton provides contrast at the bottom of the bag. **Design: Tracy Doyle**

toward the bottom. Topstitch the seam allowances to the bottom section.

5. With right sides together and ¾ inch (2 cm) seam allowance, stitch the side seams, matching upper edges and bottom seams. Overcast and topstitch as for the bag bottom.

6. To box the lower corners, fold and crease the bottom between the side seams. With the bag wrong side out, arrange each lower corner to form a point as shown, the side seam aligned with the pressed crease. Stitch across, stitching approximately 1½

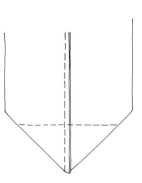

inches (4 cm) above the point and keeping the stitching line perpendicular to the seam and crease.

A Lined Tote

Adding a lining takes just a little extra time, and will make the bag sturdier. Sew a pocket to one or both sides of the lining to keep keys or sunglasses handy (see page 7 for pocket ideas).

For the lining, choose a fabric lighter in weight than that used for the outer bag. It's fun to use a contrasting pattern or color, or to decorate the lining fabric with painted or stenciled designs.

The lining is made from a single piece of fabric.

1. Cut fabric 18 inches (46 cm) wide and 27 inches (68 cm) long.

2. Fold in half across to determine placement for pockets if they will be added, keeping clear of the seam allowances on all sides. Make and stitch the pockets.

3. With right sides together and ¾ inch (2 cm) seam allowance, stitch the side seams. Overcast the seam allowances together and press to one side. Topstitch to the lining.

4. Press the upper edge ⅝ inch (1.5 cm) to the wrong side.

5. Box the corners as described in step 6 above.

6. Place the lining, wrong side out, into the finished bag. Whipstitch the folded upper edge to the bag hemline, or topstitch it in place.

A Handwoven Fabric Tote

This designer is a weaver, and made an especially durable fabric for this striking carryall. Cotton print fabric, torn into strips, is woven into a natural-colored cotton rug warp to create an unusual pattern. Cotton canvas was used for the bottom, and cotton webbing for the handles and button loop. The outer pockets were omitted, but a large patch pocket was added to each side of the soft cotton lining.

We may not all have access to handwoven fabric, but any heavy fabric will work just as well for this oversized bag. It measures approximately 15 inches (38 cm) wide, 13½ inches (34 cm) high, and 3¼ inches (8 cm) deep.

Fabric for the lining and bottom of the bag were chosen to set off the rich colors of the handwoven material. **Design: Liz Spear**

SUPPLIES

- Upper bag: ⅜ yard (.35 m) fabric, 45 inches (115 cm) or wider
- Bag bottom: ⅜ yard (.35 m) fabric, 45 inches (115 cm) or wider
- Lining fabric: ⅞ yard (.8 m). Allow additional fabric for pockets.
- Straps and button loop: 2¾ yards (2.55 m) cotton webbing, 1 inch (2.5 cm) wide
- Button: 1½ inch (4 cm) diameter

CUTTING

1. For the bag sides, cut two pieces 13 inches (33 cm) long and 19 inches (49 cm) wide.

2. Cut one piece for the bottom, 9¾ inches (25 cm) long and 19 inches (49 cm) wide.

3. Cut one lining piece 31 inches (78.5 cm) long and 19 inches (49 cm) wide. Cut pockets from lining fabric, if desired.

CONSTRUCTION

Make the lined bag as described on pages 11-12. To make the bag slightly deeper in proportion to its larger size, stitch the boxing seam (step 6) slightly farther from the point at each side seam.

For the button loop, cut a strip of webbing approximately 10 inches (25 cm) long. Fold it as shown, and stitch it into the back lining seam. Zigzag the edges together, leaving an opening just below the point to create the buttonhole.

Painted Tote

Hand-painted fabric gives the basic tote a different—and absolutely unique—character. Choose your favorite colors and decorate with stencils or outlines of any shapes you like. This designer used autumn leaves, outlining them with resist over a painted background.

For best results, begin with firmly woven 100 percent cotton fabric in white or natural. Paint will stiffen the fabric somewhat, so you can use lighter weight material than you might otherwise choose for a bag of this sort.

SUPPLIES

- Fabric, for tote sides and bottom. Refer to the yardage information and cutting instructions on page 11, but allow generous margins so the fabric can be secured for painting.
- Webbing: polyester or cotton, 1 inch (2.5 cm) wide, 2⅞ yards (2.65 m) for shoulder straps, or 2 yards (1.85 m) for shorter carrying handles.
- Fabric paints
- Cold water wax solution or other water-based resist product
- Stretcher bar frames (the kind used for artists' canvas) or a cardboard box with an opening slightly larger than the cutting dimensions of the bag side piece
- Push pins
- Small paintbrushes, sponges, and/or a foam brush
- Stencils or shapes for the designs
- Spray mister
- Unprinted newsprint or clean cloth rags and towels

PAINTING THE FABRIC

1. Wash the fabric at least twice with detergent to remove the sizing. Machine or line dry. Iron it, pressing in the direction of the lengthwise grain.

2. Cut out the bag side pieces roughly, leaving a margin of several inches on all sides to pin over the edges of the frame or box. Lightly mark the cutting lines with pencil. Cut the bottom piece and the pocket large enough to fit over the frame; mark the cutting lines.

3. Pin one fabric piece over the frame, keeping it taut and keeping the grain squared.

4. Mix paint for the background color. Follow the manufacturer's instructions and thin the paint to a runny consistency. Add texture with the sponges, if you wish. Great texture will also result if you first mist the fabric with water then paint with the foam brush. When you are satisfied with the background, remove the piece and lay it flat to dry completely.

5. Lightly trace the outlines of the designs you will use, keeping within the seamlines of each piece.

6. Place the fabric back on the frame to apply the resist. Use a small brush and outline the shapes or stencil.

7. Mix colors to paint the design shapes. This time, keep the paint slightly thicker. Apply the color as you wish—sparingly, so the background will show through, or with heavier coverage so the design areas will be opaque. Keep within the resist lines and remove excess paint from them before it dries. If you like, allow this layer of paint to dry, then lightly apply more color over it for interesting effects.

8. Allow the pieces to dry, then remove the resist. Iron the fabric between several layers of newsprint or cloth. Iron at the highest possible temperature, and change paper or cloth layers until no more of the resist comes off.

CUTTING AND CONSTRUCTION

Trim the pieces to the measurements given in the cutting instructions on page 11. Make the bag according to the instructions for the Basic Tote.

Create a custom design with a simple pattern and bright hand-painted fabric. **Pattern design: Tracy Doyle, fabric painting: Julie Sibley, bag construction: Pam Cauble**

This tote features custom-decorated straps and pocket trim. **Design: Sheri Rand**

Tote Within a Tote

Here is the chance to put your machine's decorative stitches to good use. Embroidery along the straps isn't simply pretty—it strengthens the handles besides.

This bag is made of a single length of fabric, folded cleverly to create a pocket across one side. The handles are cotton broadcloth, interfaced for stability then stitched with decorative rayon and metallic threads. A miniature version of the larger bag keeps keys or other small items away from the general clutter and within easy reach.

The outer bag is 15 inches (38 cm) wide, 12 inches (30.5 cm) high, and 6 inches (15 cm) deep. The small bag is 3½ inches (9 cm) square.

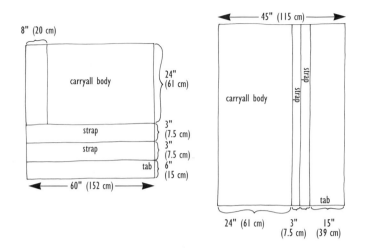

SUPPLIES

- Fabric: 1 yard (1 m) 60 inches (152 cm) wide, or 1½ yards (1.4 m) at 45 inches (115 cm)
- Fabric for straps: ¼ yard (.25 m) firmly woven muslin or comparable fabric
- Paper-backed fusible bonding web: ¾ yard (.7 m)
- Assorted decorative threads for embroidery
- Satin ribbon to match embroidery colors: 2 yards (1.85 m) each in ¼-inch and ⅛-inch (7-mm and 3-mm) widths
- Hook and loop tape: 4-inch (10-cm) strip, ½ inch (1.3 cm) wide
- Handy, but not essential: rotary cutter and mat
- Some decorative threads perform better when a special machine needle is used, for example a metafil needle for metallic threads. Check with your dealer.

CUTTING

Cut pieces according to the layout for your fabric width.

1. Cut one bag section, 24 by 52 inches (61 by 132 cm).

2. Cut two strap lining pieces, 3 by 56 to 58 inches (7.5 by 42 to 148 cm). Note that straps cut from 45-inch (115-cm) fabric will have to be pieced to the desired finished length. Cut one tab, 2½ by 5 inches (6.5 by 13 cm).

3. For the mini bag, cut one piece 5½ by 14 inches (14 by 36 cm).

CONSTRUCTION

1. Serge or overcast the two long edges of the bag piece. Fold the piece in half across so that it measures 24 by 26 inches (61 by 66 cm). Press the fold to crease it.

2. Make the strip for the pocket edge and handles. Bond fusible web to the wrong side of the muslin fabric. Cut three strips 1¼ inches (3.25 cm) wide. Remove the paper backing. Cut one strip to 24 inches (61 cm) for the pocket trim.

3. Press in place approximately ⅛ inch (3 mm) inside the folded edge.

4. Fold the side edges of the strap sections toward center, wrong sides together. Press firmly in place. Bond strips of muslin to each strap section to cover the raw edges.

5. Work decorative stitching along each strap, starting with a row along the center of the strip and working toward the outer edges. Press gently on the wrong side of the strip to set the stitches, tugging slightly to straighten the piece.

6. To make the pocket, bring the decorated folded edge upward to form a pocket 9½ inches (24 cm) deep as shown. Press the lower fold. Machine baste along each side.

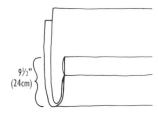

9½" (24cm)

7. Lay the bag flat, right side up. Chalk mark placement lines for the straps 6½ inches (17 cm) in from each side. Mark the vertical center of the piece; this will be the bottom of the bag.

8. Position the straps. Start with an end at the bag bottom and center the strap length over one marked line, leaving a loop extending beyond the upper edge to form the handle, down along the other marked line, the remaining end at the bottom of the bag. Pin the other strap to the other end of the bag, abutting the ends against the ends of the first strap.

9. Pin and stitch the straps close to each edge, ending the stitching 5 inches (13 cm) from the bag upper edge. Using satin stitch, stitch over the end joins at the bag bottom.

10. Fold the piece with right sides together and upper edges even. Stitch the side seams with ½ inch (1.5 cm) seam allowance. Stitch again ⅛ inch (3 mm) away in the seam allowance.

11. To box the lower corners, press a crease across the bottom between the ends of the side seams. Fold each corner to a point, the side seam aligned with the pressed line. Chalk mark a line across the point, exactly perpendicular to the crease and seam, 3 inches (7.5 cm) from the point. Stitch across the marked line (see the drawing on page 12).

12. Make the tab. Press the long raw edges of the tab piece ½ inch (1.3 cm) to the wrong side. Fold the piece in half and press again. Fold in ½ inch (1.3 cm) at one end; press.

13. For the hem, serge or overcast the upper edge of the bag. Fold under 1¼ inches (3 cm); press. Place the tab at center back, the unfinished end under the edge of the hem, and baste it in place. Stitch the hem.

A replica of the larger bag, the attached mini tote keeps small items within reach.

14. Finishing. Reinforce stitch the tab. Stitch the remaining strap sections. Reinforce the upper ends of the straps by stitching an X on each one in the bag hem area.

15. Make the mini bag. Center the narrow ribbon along the wider one and stitch in place along both edges with a decorative or zigzag stitch.

16. Fold the bag piece in half, right side out, and press the fold. Fold this edge upward 2¼ inches (6 cm) to form the pocket.

17. Serge or overcast the short ends of the piece. Cut a piece of the decorated strap ribbon 33 inches (84 cm) long. Stitch it along each end of the bag, the ribbon edge 1 inch (2.5 cm) from the fabric edge.

18. With right sides together, stitch *one* side seam. Open out and stitch a ½-inch (1.5-cm) hem at the upper edge. Stitch the other side seam.

19. Attach the hook and loop tape along the hem at each side of the bag.

20. Use the remaining double ribbon to attach the mini bag to the large bag as shown in the photo.

Backpacks & Rucksacks

Rucksacks, backpacks, and their kin are designed for performance, ready to be filled with all the necessities for a day's trek in the mountains or a week of travel through Europe. A recent adaptation of the style is the city pack, dressed up and scaled down for urban treks to and from the office. Bags like these can carry a heavy load with ease because the weight is distributed evenly across the shoulders.

Sturdy, durable fabric is the best choice for these bag styles. The material should be strong enough that it won't give way, and stable enough that it won't stretch out of shape. The models on the following pages illustrate a wide range of fabric options, from traditional nylon to stylish hemp and gabardine. Durability is a criterion for the trimmings, too. Strap materials, lining, and closures should stand up to heavy use and last as long as the outer fabric.

Sewing techniques play a large part in creating a long-wearing pack. Double-stitched hems, topstitching, and serged or double-sewn seams like French seams all help strenghten the bag. Look over the sewing tips in the Introduction for more suggestions.

Traditional styling and materials are combined in a pack that will see years of service. **Design: Dee Dee Triplett**

Almost Bottomless Backpack

This is a sturdy and spacious bag, scaled to carry all you need for a day in the city or—if you pack efficiently—a weekend in Rio. It zips down both sides of the front for easy access to the contents. A security strap prevents access to the pack while it is being worn.

A large removable inner pocket has a zippered compartment and assorted smaller pouches along the front to keep small items organized. On the inner front flap is another large pocket, with expansion pleats and a hook and loop tape closure. Interior straps hold a water bottle or pair of shoes in place at the sides of the pack.

The appliqué on the front flap alludes to the turtle from the Lakota legend who carried his house on his back. You may add your own significant design to the flap, or stitch on a few interesting patches or decorative buttons.

We have used durable materials for this bag, intending it to last for generations. The fabric and findings are the kinds used for outdoor equipment and can be found in camping supply stores or from mail order sources that advertise in sewing magazines.

The backpack is 12 inches (30.5 cm) wide, 15½ inches (39.5 cm) high, and 5 inches (12.5 cm) deep.

SUPPLIES

- Fabric: 1⅜ yards (1.35 m) 1000 denier Cordura
- Nylon webbing, 1 inch (2.5 cm) wide: one 12-inch (31-cm) length and two 48-inch (122-cm) lengths, the ends heat sealed
- Nylon webbing, ½ inch (1.3 cm) wide: three 24-inch (61-cm) lengths, the ends heat sealed
- Ladder locks: two, 1 inch (2.5 cm) wide
- Side release buckles: one, 1 inch (2.5 cm) wide; and three, ½ inch (1.3 cm) wide
- Separating sport zippers: two, 14 inches (35 cm) long
- Standard separating zippers: two, 12 inches (30.5 cm) long

- Grosgrain ribbon: ¼ yard (.25 m), ¾ inch (2 cm) wide
- Hook and loop tape: ½ yard (.5 m), ¾ inch (2 cm) wide
- Double fold bias tape: 2 yards (1.85 m)
- For the flap appliqué: scrap of synthetic suede, 8 inches (20 cm) square
- Paper backed fusible web for appliqué
- Machine needles: sharp, coated jeans needles work well with Cordura

CUTTING

Cordura does not ravel, so seams and hems are left unfinished except where they are visible in order to reduce bulk. If you use another material you may need to adjust cutting sizes of some of the pieces to allow for double hems.

1. Enlarge the pattern pieces on pages 46-47 and cut them out.

2. From the patterns, cut 1 top, 1 bottom, 1 inner front pocket flap, and 2 front flaps (one will be the lining).

3. Cut one inner front pocket, 15¼ by 13 inches (38.5 by 33 cm).

4. Cut one pack front, 17 inches (43 cm) square.

5. Cut one pack back/sides piece, 25 by 17 inches (63.5 by 43 cm).

6. Cut one top band strip, 6 by 42 inches (15.25 by 106.5 cm).

7. Cut one top hinge, 8 by 13 inches (20 by 33 cm).

8. Cut one inner pocket, 13½ by 29½ inches (34 by 75 cm).

9. For the custom pouches on the inner pocket, cut one piece 5½ by 16 inches (14 by 41 cm).

CONSTRUCTION

For ease in construction, work with the pieces flat as long as is possible.

Pack Front and Front Pocket

1. Hem one side (the top) of the front inner pocket piece with a 1-inch (2.5-cm) single hem. On the right side of fabric, sew a 4-inch (10-cm) length of the loop section of the hook and loop tape, centering it approximately 3¾ inches (9.5 cm) down from top. Set aside.

2. On the 17-inch (43-cm) sides of the pack front, turn under 1 inch (2.5 cm) and press lightly to "score" the fabric. Turn under 1½ inches (4 cm) on one short side (the top) and press the same way. These scored lines will serve as guides later. Sew a 5-inch (12.5-cm) strip of the hook section of the hook and loop tape to the right side of the piece at the center, 7½ inches (19 cm) up from the bottom.

3. Open the scored top and side hems. With right sides together and bottoms even, sew the pocket to the front with ½ inch (1.5 cm) seam allowance. Now you have a tube. Turn right side out. Match centers of the bottoms.

4. Fold a pleat toward each side of the pocket to fit the bottom of the pocket to the front section. Stitch the pieces together. Leave raw edges out.

5. Attach one 14-inch (35-cm) separating zipper to each side. Have the pack front pocket side up, the zipper right side down. Beginning 1 inch (2.5 cm) from the bottom, nestle the zipper teeth along the side seam, keeping the front section folded along the pressed lines so that the zipper will be covered when the front is closed. Sew the zipper to within a few inches from the top. At the top, cut off extra teeth above the zipper

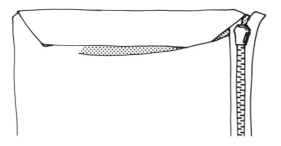

stop. Fold the upper hem diagonally over the end of the zipper tape to tuck into the pocket as shown and, if necessary, cut away a section of side turn-under. Turn under the raw edge of the back/side hem approximately ¼ inch (.5 cm) where the zipper stitching will cross it. Finish the stitching, catching part of the hem as you sew. Repeat for the second zipper on the other side.

6. Make the inner pocket flap. Turn under and press ½ inch (1.5 cm) on five sides, leaving the longest side (the top) unhemmed. Stitch. With right sides together, line up unhemmed flap top with the raw edge at top of the pack front. Stitch approximately ¼ inch (.7 cm) from the edges, and again 1 inch (2.5 cm) from the edges. Reinforce by sewing a box shape at the side hemlines between the seamlines. Stitch the other hook and loop tape section to the underside of pocket flap to correspond to the piece on the pocket. Apply seam binding over the flap/front seam if desired.

Back and Sides

1. On the back/side piece, press under ½ inch (1.5 cm) on the two 17-inch (43-cm) sides and 1½ inches (4 cm) on one longer side (the top), as you did for the pack front.

2. Attach the other halves of the 14-inch (35-cm) zippers to the sides. With the right side of one side of the piece facing you, position the zipper underneath, the fold of the fabric close to the zipper teeth. Make sure the bottom of this piece is aligned with the bottom of the front. Sew to within a few inches of the top. Finish at the top as for the front. Repeat for the other side. Hint: unzip the finished side completely so the piece will lie flat.

Pack top

1. Fold the top band strip in half lengthwise, right side out, and press lightly.

2. Beginning at the back side of the top approximately 2 inches (5 cm) from a corner and leaving 1 inch (2.5 cm) of the band unsewn, sew the doubled raw edges around the pack top, right sides together and with ½ inch (1.5 cm) seam allowance. Clip curves to ease around corners. When you are close to finishing, trim the unsewn end of the band to fit inside the

Appliqué a favorite motif on the front flap to personalize your pack.

folded band at the beginning and continue sewing. Stitch down along the fold where the ends join to prevent the band from spreading apart.

Front Flap

1. If desired, fuse and stitch the appliqué to one flap section, or embellish as you wish.

2. On the remaining flap section (the lining), stitch the other section of the 5-inch (12.5-cm) hook and loop tape piece to correspond to the strip on the pack front. Allow slight ease so the pieces will line up when the pack is filled.

3. For carriers for the security strap, cut the grosgrain ribbon in half. Fold each piece double and stitch one to each side of the flap lining, approximately ¾ inch (2 cm) from each side seamline and with the ends approximately ⅝ inch (1.5 cm) below the hook and loop tape, toward the rounded end of the flap. Stitch the ends of each carrier firmly, making sure the 1-inch (2.5-cm) webbing will pass through them.

4. Sew the flap to the lining with right sides together and ½ inch (1.5 cm) seam allowance along the two long edges and rounded end, leaving the top end open. Clip curves, turn right sides out.

5. The flap is sewn behind the pack top band at center front. Line up the flap raw edges with those of the band. Stitch in the ditch of the top/band seam, and again along the edge of the band.

6. Make the hinge to join the top and back. Fold the hinge piece in half lengthwise, right side out. Sew both 4-inch (10-cm) ends closed; turn right side out. Place the piece under the back of the top band, matching raw edges, and sew in the ditch as for the front flap.

7. To attach the hinge to the pack, center and line up the seamline at the top/hinge with the folded upper edge of the pack back. Stitch across, ¼ inch (.5 cm) from the *lower edge* of the hinge and again approximately ⅜ inch (1 cm) above the first stitching line. The hinge will be stitched again after the inner pocket is in place.

A separating zipper at each side of the pack front permits easy access to the contents and the inner pockets. The top flap fastens to the pack front with hook and loop tape. On the underside of the flap, grosgrain ribbon carriers hold the security strap in place.

Removable Inner Pocket

The large inner pocket attaches to the upper back of the pack with a separating zipper. The pocket itself has a zippered compartment as well as organizer pouches across the front. The organizer section can be customized to hold the items you will store in it. Lay out those pieces on the completed pocket, place the pouch strip over them, and mark placement of the vertical stitching lines where you need them. Fold a small pleat at the bottom of any compartment that will hold a bulky item.

1. On the pouch strip, fold under both long edges ½ inch (1.5 cm). Press one fold firmly, then stitch the hem. This will be the pocket top. Press the other fold lightly.

2. On the large pocket piece, mark placement lines for the pouch strip. Mark parallel lines across the 13½-inch (34-cm) width, one line 2¾ inches (7 cm) down from the top, the second 4½ inches (11.5 cm) below the first.

3. Press under ½ inch (1.5 cm) on the left end of the pouch strip. Position on the large piece between the lines, keeping at least 1 inch (2.5 cm) from the edge of the large piece. Stitch close to the pressed fold. Fit the strip over the items it will contain. Make pleats at the bottom of the strip as necessary, and mark vertical stitching lines. End the strip with a folded edge at least 1 inch (2.5 cm) from the right side of the pocket. Stitch across the bottom and along the remaining side.

4. Install the zipper. Place a 12-inch (30.5-cm) zipper face down along the upper edge of the pocket right side, lining up the zipper tape with pocket edge. Stitch close to the teeth on the side nearest the pocket edge. Fold up the bottom of the pocket and sew other side of zipper across that end in the same way. Fold a pleat approximately ¾ inch (2 cm) to overlap the zipper as for a garment and stitch it along the zipper tape. Turn the pocket wrong side out. Open the zipper part way.

A large interior pocket unzips to go into a purse or glove compartment. Its exterior pouches can be sized to accommodate your own essentials.

5. Fold the pocket so that the zipper is 1½ to 1¾ inches (4 cm) below the top fold on side with the pouches. Sew both side seams with ½ inch (1.5 cm) seam allowance.

6. One last zipper! The remaining 12-inch (30.5-cm) zipper attaches the pocket to the upper pack back. Unfold the hem at the pack upper edge. Center the zipper, face down, along the edge of the pack, aligning the zipper tape edge with the fabric edge. Stitch near the zipper teeth. Turn the zipper to the right side and stitch again, this time stitch-

ing through both fabric layers to hem the pack at the same time, but not stitching through the band. Stitch the remainder of the hem beyond the ends of the zipper. Smooth down the top band, and stitch again along the zipper area through all thicknesses.

7. Sew the remaining zipper tape to the top of the detachable pocket, the folded upper edge of the pocket close to the zipper teeth with both right side up. Leave the pocket detached.

Straps adjust for fit around the body. At the upper back is a handle. A security strap slips through a carrier on the underside of the front flap then fastens around the pack.

Attaching the Straps

1. For the handle, position the shorter length of 1-inch (2.5-cm) webbing on the band at the pack back as shown below.

2. Pin the remaining two strap lengths as shown, placing the handle ends under the straps at the upper back. Try on the pack and adjust the straps to fit your body.

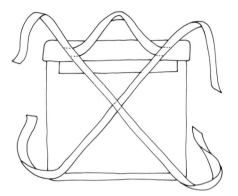

3. Sew the straps to the pack body, starting 1 inch (2.5 cm) above the pack bottom. Sew to approximately ½ inch (1.5 cm) above the lower edge of the top band. Take care not to sew over the last zipper. Stitch double lines across the straps at the top of the band to keep the pack upright on your back.

Finishing

1. The pack is still bottomless—let's fix that. Mark centers of the long sides of the pack bottom. Zip the pack front onto the bag, but leave off the detachable inner pocket. Match centers of the bottom piece to center front and back of the pack. Stitch, right sides together, with ½ inch (1.5 cm) seam allowance. Clip corners. Turn right side out.

2. To keep the top closed and in place, sew a 2½-inch (6.5-cm) strip of hook and loop tape at the top of the pack at each side, and to the underside of the top band.

3. For the interior restraining straps to hold a water bottle or pair of shoes, cut the narrow webbing into thirds, or as desired. Apply ladder locks to the ends of the strips.

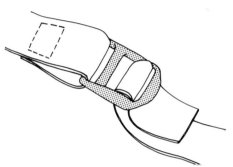

4. On the inside of the pack, position the strips with their midpoints at the midpoint of the side section. Place one halfway up on one side. Place two on the other side, about one-third of the way from the pack top and bottom. Stitch each strap in place at its center with a square or X.

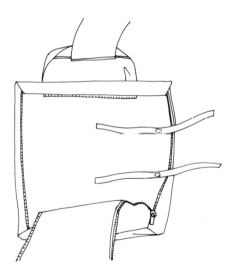

5. For a finished appearance inside, bind the visible seam allowances around the inner top of the bag (the lower ones too, if you wish) with seam binding.

With its distinctive appearance and tremendous capacity, this pack is a traveler's favorite companion. **Design: Sheri Rand**

Hemp Rucksack

I ts stylish good looks are deceptive. Made in durable hemp fabric, this bag is designed to last for years. And when the fabrics are preshrunk, it can be laundered as often as necessary.

The finished bag is 15½ inches (39 cm) wide and 19 inches (48 cm) high, providing plenty of room for weekend gear. A front gusset allows for tightening up the bag's circumference when the load is smaller, and provides an interesting design element at the same time. The top is gathered closed with cords that continue through a channel on the flap lining and tie through the upper loops on the front gusset. The bag is interlined for durability and to provide a sturdy backing for pockets on the lining.

The wide straps are padded for comfort. The D-ring attachment allows for length adjustment.

There are plenty of options for adding your own original touch. To lace up the front, make twisted cord from strands of leftover yarns. Try contrasting trim along the lacing panel as the designer did for the bag shown on page 35. Piece sturdy fabrics for an intriguing patchwork bag. This designer used a bright calico lining to contrast with the neutral hemp fabric, and a subtle striped shirting with the tapestry version on page 35.

SUPPLIES

- Fabric for outer bag: 1¼ yards (1.15 m), fairly heavy weight
- Lining fabric: 1¼ yards (1.15 m)
- Interlining: garment weight batting or firmly woven cotton, 21 by 32 inches (53 by 81 cm)
- Thick batting for shoulder straps: two strips 2 by 24 inches (5 by 61 cm)
- Cording: 3 yards (2.75 m)
- D-rings: Four, 1-inch (2.5-cm) diameter

CUTTING

1. Enlarge the pattern pieces on page 48 and cut them from paper.

2. Cut one bag body from outer fabric, 21 by 35 inches (53 by 89 cm).

3. Cut bag body lining, 21 by 32 inches (53 by 81 cm).

4. With the pattern, cut one flap and one bottom section from outer fabric and from lining.

5. From outer fabric, cut two shoulder straps, 5 by 24 inches (12.5 by 61 cm). Cut two lower extension straps 3 by 9 inches (7.5 by 23 cm).

6. For the gusset cord loops, cut a strip from outer fabric, 1½ by 29 inches (4 by 73 cm).

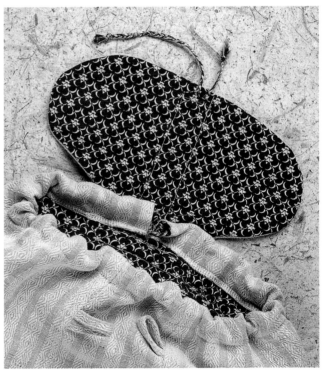

Colorful calico provides a nice contrast to the neutral shade of the hemp fabric. The drawcord around the top of the bag slips through a channel on the underside of the flap, then through the empty loops at the upper front of the bag.

7. From lining fabric, cut one cord channel piece, 2 by 5 inches (5 by 12.5 cm).

8. If desired, cut pockets from lining fabric.

CONSTRUCTION

Use ½ inch (1.5 cm) seam allowance except as noted.

1. On the bag body, mark the center, top and bottom, of the 35-inch (89-cm) side. This is center front. Chalk mark a line from top to bottom 2 inches (5 cm) each side of center front. Mark another line 1½ inches (4 cm) outside each of the first two.

2. Make the gusset loops. Fold the strip in half lengthwise, right side out, and press. Fold the long edges in ¼ inch (.5 cm); press. Stitch along both long edges. Cut the strip into eight 2½-inch (6.5-cm) pieces and two 4-inch (10-cm) pieces.

3. Fold the strips in half and position them on the bag body front. Place the two longer strips opposite each other 4 inches (10 cm) from the upper edge of the bag, the strip seamlines along the inner marked lines, the folds toward center. Position the remaining loops at 2½-inch (6.5-cm) intervals. Stitch securely in place across the ends of the loops.

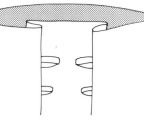

4. On the outside of the bag body, crease along each outer chalk line and fold it toward the center of the piece to meet each inner chalk line, covering the ends of the loops. Edgestitch along each fold on the outside. Stitch again approximately ½ inch (1.5 cm) away, catching the inner pleat.

5. Stitch the center back seam, right sides together, stopping 2½ inches (6.5 cm) from the top. Press open.

6. Make the lower extension straps. Fold the strips lengthwise, right side out, approximately into thirds

with the long edges overlapping slightly. Stitch through all thicknesses with a wide, close zigzag stitch to encase the raw edge. Turn under ⅜ inch (1 cm) at one end of each strap and zigzag the same way.

7. Position the straps on the bag back, wrong side up, the unfinished ends 5 inches (12.5 cm) to either side of center and 1½ inches (4 cm) above the lower edge of the bag. Place them at approximately a 45-degree angle as shown. Stitch across each end with a close zigzag. Flip the straps upward and stitch again with a straight stitch to enclose the raw ends.

8. Machine baste interlining to the wrong side of the main lining and lining bottom pieces, stitching in the seam allowances.

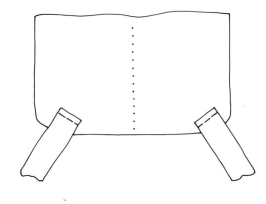

9. For lining pockets, hem one edge of the pocket section(s) and press under the remaining edges. Topstitch the front pocket in place on the lining, the top approximately 6 inches (15 cm) from the bag upper edge.

10. Fold the lining, right sides together, and stitch as for the bag. Add a pocket over the center back if desired.

11. Set in the bag and lining bottom pieces. Fold the bag, matching center front and back seam, to mark the sides. Mark the lining in the same way. Mark centers and sides on the bottom pieces. Stitch the bag bottom in place, right sides together, clipping around curves as necessary. Stitch the lining bottom.

The back straps are wide, and are padded with batting for comfort. Lower extension straps permit adjustment for length.

12. Secure the lining to the bag around the bottom. Match the bottom of the outer bag to the bottom of the lining with wrong sides together. Make sure the back seamlines are also matched. Stitch together ⅛ inch (3 mm) outside the previous stitching line. Turn right side out.

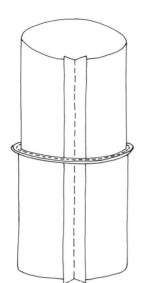

13. On the unstitched portion of the upper back seam, press under the bag and lining seam allowances. Edgestitch the bag to the lining along both sides of the opening.

14. Clean finish the upper bag and lining edges together. Press and stitch a 1½-inch (4-cm) hem, leaving the ends open. This will be the cord channel.

15. Make the flap. Fold under ¼ inch (.5 cm) at each short end of the flap channel piece; press and stitch. Fold under both long edges the same way; press. Center the piece, right side up, on the flap lining right side with one short end approximately 1½ inches (4 cm) from the flap straight edge (see the drawing at step 16). Stitch close to both long edges. Stitch the outer and lining flap sections with right sides together around the curved edge using ⅜ inch (1 cm) seam allowance. Trim; turn. Topstitch if desired.

16. Make the shoulder straps. Taper one end of each batting strip. At the end, cut ½ inch (1.3 cm) from the long edge at each side, tapering to the original edge about 2½ inches (6.5 cm) up. Center a batting strip on

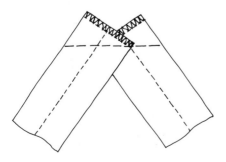

the wrong side of each strap. Fold the strap around the batting, and fold under the overlapping raw edge. Stitch through all layers with a zigzag stitch, encasing the overlapping edge of the strap. Clean finish the straight ends. Pull each tapered end through a pair of D-rings, folding the end up approximately 1 inch (2.5 cm). Zigzag the end to the strap. Overlap the shoulder straps, wrong sides up, as shown. Stitch across them. Fold under along the stitching line; press.

17. With both pieces right side up, position the flap on the bag back. Place the seamline of the flap straight edge along the stitching line of the bag hem, or approximately 1¼ inches (3 cm) below the bag upper edge. Place the folded edge of the straps on top, the fold along the flap seamline. Stitch close to the strap folded edge. Stitch again ¾ inch (2 cm) below the first stitching line. Thread the lower extension straps through the D-rings.

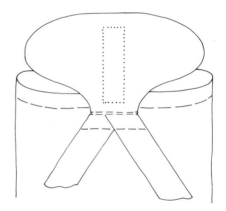

18. Cut the cord in half. Knot the ends to prevent fraying. Thread one length through the upper casing and both ends through the flap casing. When the top is gathered closed, the cord ends are pulled through the upper two loops on the front gusset and tied together. Thread the remaining cord length through the lower eight gusset loops as shown in the photo, beginning and ending at the bottom.

Tapestry Rucksack

Tapestry upholstery fabric works beautifully for this design. It is strong and durable—and it won't show dirt. The contrast trim is heavy cotton, but purchased trim could be used instead. Be sure to buy an uncoated fabric; the rubbery backing applied to some upholstery materials makes stitching difficult. The bag is made like the hemp rucksack, page 29, but with a few differences.

CUTTING

1. Cut the bag main body piece and the lining 21 by 32 inches (53 by 81 cm).

2. Cut two strips for the front gusset trim, 2 by 21 inches (5 by 53 cm).

The lower extension straps also are made from the contrast fabric. For lining, striped cotton shirting repeats the tapestry colors and provides another texture.

3. Cut strips for the gusset loops and lower extension straps from the trim fabric.

4. Cut remaining pieces according to the instructions on page 29.

CONSTRUCTION

1. Because trim is added to the front, pleats are not used along the gusset. On the main bag body piece, chalk mark a line 2 inches (5 cm) to either side of center, from top to bottom of the piece.

2. Fold the long edges of each trim strip to center, right side out, and press firmly.

3. Make the gusset loops and position them as described in steps 2 and 3, page 30. Place the trim strips so that the inner folded edges just cover the chalked lines. Edgestitch along both edges, covering the ends of the loops.

4. Complete the bag as for the hemp bag.

Contrast trim and cords add colorful accents on the tapestry version of the bag. **Design: Sheri Rand**

A tailored gabardine city pack works equally well with business attire and casual clothes. **Design: Dawn Anderson**

City Pack

I t's made in the rucksack style, tailored and trimmed down to work with a business suit or dress. This one is wool gabardine, a fabric not usually associated with a bag of this sort but that sews up beautifully and maintains a neat appearance.

The lined bag is constructed of separate front, back, and side pieces. Plastic mesh stiffens and strengthens the bottom, and corded piping gives a finished look around the lower edge. A drawcord threads through eyelets in the upper band to close the top. Buckles allow for length adjustment at both ends of the handle, and the shoulder straps adjust by means of slides. On the front, a patch pocket keeps keys or other small items within easy reach. Pockets could easily be added to the lining, too, with just a little extra time and fabric.

The finished bag is 9½ inches (24 cm) wide and 11½ inches (29 cm) high.

SUPPLIES

- Outer fabric: ⅞ yard (.8 m)
- Lining: ⅜ yard (.35 m)
- Fusible interfacing to suit fabric: 1 yard (1 m)
- Fusible waistband interfacing, 1¼ inches (3.2 cm) wide and 27 inches (68.5 cm) long
- Plastic mesh, 9½ by 5½ inches (24 by 14 cm)
- Piping cord: 2½ yards (2.3 m), ¼ inch (7 mm) diameter
- Eyelets: twelve, ¼ inch (7 mm) diameter; six, ⅛ inch (3 mm) diameter
- Eyelet tool
- Slides for back straps: four, 1-inch (2.5-cm) width
- Handle buckles: two, 1-inch (2.5-cm) width
- Optional, for finishing the drawcord ends: Two ¼-inch (7-mm) diameter end caps, two small metal jump rings, and two metal charms to hang from end caps, cyanoacrylate glue.

CUTTING

Seam allowance of ½ inch (1.3 cm) is included in pattern pieces and measurements except as otherwise noted.

1. Enlarge the pattern pieces on page 48 and cut them from paper.

2. For the bag front and back, cut two pieces from outer fabric, lining, and interfacing, 11 inches (28 cm) long and 10 inches (25.5 cm) wide.

3. For bag sides, cut two pieces from outer fabric and lining, and four from interfacing: 11 inches (28 cm) long and 5 inches (12.5 cm) wide.

4. Cut two back strap pieces from outer fabric, 30½ inches (77.5 cm) long and 3¼ inches (8.5 cm) wide. Cut two pieces of interfacing this width and 1 inch (2.5 cm) shorter. Cut two back strap attachment loops from outer fabric, 3 inches (7.5 cm) long and 3¼ inches (8.5 cm) wide. Cut two strips of interfacing this size.

5. For the handle, cut two pieces from outer fabric and two from interfacing, 19 inches (48 cm) long and 2⅛ inches (5.5 cm) wide. Using the template, trim the ends of each piece to a point. Cut two buckle tabs from outer fabric and from interfacing, 4 inches (10 cm) long and 3¼ inches (8.5 cm) wide.

6. Cut the bag upper band from outer fabric on the straight grain, 27 inches (68.5 cm) long and 3¾ inches (9.5 cm) wide.

7. For piping around the bag bottom, cut a bias strip from outer fabric, 28 inches (71 cm) long and 1½ inches (4 cm) wide. For the drawcord, cut a strip on the straight grain, 30 by 2 inches (76 by 5 cm).

8. Cut a front pocket piece 4¾ by 5¾ inches (12 by 14.5 cm), and cut interfacing the same size.

CONSTRUCTION

1. Following the manufacturer's instructions, fuse interfacing to the wrong sides of the bag front, back, and side sections. Apply the additional piece to each side section. Apply the interfacing to the back strap pieces so that 1 inch (2.5 cm) at an end of each piece is not interfaced. Apply interfacing to all other pieces.

2. Make the pocket. Fold the piece with right sides together, aligning the two short ends. Stitch the seam just at each end, leaving the center open for turning. Fold the piece so that the seam is approximately ¾ inch (2 cm) to one side. Stitch the ends. Trim; turn. Whipstitch the opening. Topstitch along the ditch formed by the seam to simulate a hem. Center the pocket on the bag front with the bottom approximately 3 inches (7.5 cm) above the bag lower edge. Edgestitch in place.

3. Join the bag front, side, and back sections, stitching with right sides together. Press each seam open and topstitch ⅛ inch (3 mm) from the seam on each side.

4. Fold each back strap section in half lengthwise, wrong side out, and stitch the long edges and across the uninterfaced end. Trim and turn. Stitch the long edges of the attachment loop pieces; turn. Edgestitch the long edges of all pieces.

5. Slip each attachment loop over the lower bar of a slide. Baste the raw ends together. Fold the finished end of each back strap around the center of one of the remaining metal slides, from the back. Stitch the strap end in place, approximately ⅝ inch (1.5 cm) from the bar. Slip the other end of each strap through the upper loop of the slide with the attachment loop, then from back to front over the center bar of the slide to which the other strap end is sewn.

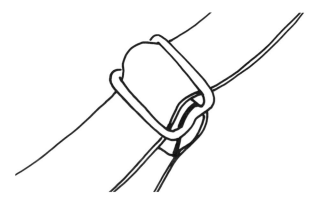

6. Baste the strap ends in place at the center of the bag upper edge, approximately ¾ inch (2 cm) apart. Taking care not to twist the straps, baste the ends of the attachment loops to the bag lower edge, 4 inches (10 cm) apart.

7. Make the piping. Fold the bias strip right side out around the cording and stitch close to the cord. Pin to the right side of the bag bottom, raw edges together and seamlines matched. Clip the piping seam allowance around curves as necessary. Overlap the ends by about 1 inch (2.5 cm). Stitch in place, leaving about 2 inches (5 cm) unstitched at the ends. Remove the stitching at one end of the piping and trim the cord so the cord ends meet. Fold under ½ inch (1.3 cm) of fabric and fold it around the remaining end of the piping. Finish the stitching.

8. Quarter-mark the bag bottom with pins, and mark the upper bag piece in the same way. Pin the bottom in place with right sides together. Stitch just inside the piping stitching line.

9. On the paper pattern for the bottom, trim away the seam allowance and an additional 1/16 inch (2 mm) or so. Cut the plastic mesh to this size. Fit the mesh into the bottom of the bag and stitch it by hand to the seam allowances.

10. Make the buckle tabs. Fold each piece lengthwise and stitch the long edges and across one end. Trim, turn, and press. Edgestitch the long edges. Make a ⅜-inch (1-cm) buttonhole in the center of each piece, 1⅜ inch (3.5 cm) from the unfinished end. Fold each piece over a buckle slide, the tab through the buttonhole, so that the finished end extends approximately 1 inch (2.5 cm) beyond the raw end. Center a tab on each side section of the bag, the center bar of the buckle even with the upper edge of the bag. Edgestitch the tab ends in place with a square, catching the raw edge of the tab in the stitching.

11. Make the lining. Stitch the front, back, and side pieces together as for the outer bag. Staystitch the bottom piece ⅜ inch (1 cm) from the edge and clip to the stitching around the curves. Stitch to the upper bag. Press. Pin into the bag with wrong sides together and baste around the upper edge.

12. Apply the waistband interfacing to the edge band wrong side, placing it within the seamline on one long edge. Stitch the short ends of the band with right sides together; press open. Press under the seam allowance on the long edge of the uninterfaced side of the band.

13. Quarter-mark the band and the upper edge of the bag. Stitch the band to the bag upper edge, right sides together, along the interfacing stitching line. Trim seam allowances and press toward the band. Fold the pressed edge of the band to the inside to just cover the previous stitching. Edgestitch from the right side, catching the inner folded edge. Edgestitch the upper edge.

14. Mark positions for the twelve larger eyelets around the center of the band, placing two about 2¼ inches (5.5 cm) apart at center front and back then spacing the remainder evenly. Attach the eyelets.

15. Make the handle. Stitch the interfaced sections with right sides together, leaving an opening for turning. Trim, turn, and press. Edgestitch. Attach three smaller eyelets at each end of the handle. Place the first approximately 3 inches (7.5 cm) from the ends and space the others approximately 1 inch (2.5 cm) apart.

16. Make the drawcord. Fold the fabric strip, wrong side out, around a length of cord twice the fabric length, with the pieces even at one end. Stitch securely across the end of the cord and fabric, then along the fabric long edges, taking care not to catch the cord in the stitching. Trim and zigzag the long edges. Turn right side out over the cord. Trim away the exposed cord. Thread the cord through the bag band. Finish the ends by gluing the end caps in place and attaching the charms. As an alternative, clip away ⅝ inch (1.5 cm) of the cord inside each end, turn the fabric to the inside, and hand stitch the ends. Knot the ends to keep them in place.

Metal slides provide for lengthening or shortening the back straps. The bottom of the bag is reinforced with plastic mesh and trimmed with corded piping.

Suede City Pack

Synthetic suede in jewel colors gives the city pack a very different character, and it is every bit as useful. To work in still more color or to add design lines, piece the front, back, and sides from smaller scraps.

The bag is made according to the instructions that begin on page 39. Because this material is quite stable and does not ravel, some construction shortcuts can be taken. It isn't necessary to interface the bag front, back, and sides. It is a good idea to use a light, firm interfacing in the handle, straps, and edge band to prevent stretching and to provide reinforcement for the eyelets. These pieces could be cut without seam allowances and edgestitched together, right sides out.

The plastic mesh can be omitted from the bottom. Lining also could be omitted, but it makes for a nicely finished bag and provides a place to add interior pockets if you wish.

Colorful synthetic suede makes a pack that is fun to use and still very practical. **Pack design: Dawn Anderson; this model by Mary Parker**

Natural linen makes a hard-working backpack that is elegant besides. **Design: Lori Kerr**

Backpack in Linen

Made of long-lasting linen and trimmed in synthetic leather, this spacious pack is as sturdy as it is pretty to look at. Best of all, it can be thrown into the washer if the trip takes its toll. The body of the pack is backed with fusible interfacing—in black to match the trim. The bottom is synthetic leather, durable and soil resistant.

The finished pack is approximately 14 inches (35.5 cm) wide, 19 inches (48 cm) high, and 4 inches (10 cm) deep exclusive of the cargo pocket. The back straps are adjustable, and are reinforced with webbing. A handle at the upper back makes for easy carrying when the bag is off the shoulders.

On the outside, the large upper pocket has a wide flap that snaps at both corners. The lower cargo pocket zips closed from both ends for easy access to all the small essentials. Inside is another zippered pocket for secure storage of the passport, tickets, and cash.

SUPPLIES

- Linen fabric, medium to heavy weight: 1 yard (1 m), 60 inches (152 cm) wide
- Fusible tricot interfacing: 1 yard (1 m), 60 inches (152 cm) wide
- Synthetic leather or suede: ¼ yard (.25 m)
- Webbing, cotton or polyester: 2⅛ yards (1.95 m), 1 inch (2.5 cm) wide
- Two decorative or sports zippers, 20 inches (50.5 cm) long
- Three 9-inch (23-cm) zippers
- Four slides, 1½ inches (3.8 cm) wide
- Two large snaps

CUTTING

If you plan to wash the pack, preshrink fabrics before cutting.

1. For the pack front and back, cut two pieces from linen and two from interfacing, 14 by 20 inches (35.5 by 50.5 cm).

2. Cut synthetic leather and interfacing for the bottom, 20 by 5 inches (51 by 12.5 cm). Cut two leather pieces, 6 by 2 inches (15 by 5 cm), for strap end reinforcements.

3. Cut two zipper gusset strips from linen, 44 by 5½ inches (112 by 14 cm).

4. Cut two back straps from linen, 30 by 2½ inches (76 by 6.5 cm). Cut linen for the handle, 13 by 4 inches (33 by 10 cm). Cut a strip of webbing the length of each of these three pieces.

5. For the lower cargo pocket, cut linen and interfacing 10 by 7 inches (25.5 by 17.5 cm). Cut two linen strips for the zipper gusset, 22 by 4½ inches (56 by 11.5 cm). For the bottom, cut two pieces from linen and two from interfacing, 9 by 4½ inches (23 by 11.5 cm).

6. For the upper pocket, cut two pieces from linen and one from interfacing, 10½ by 7 inches (26.5 by 18 cm). Cut two flap sections from linen and one from interfacing, 11¼ by 7 inches (28.5 by 18 cm). Cut a leather strip ¾ by 10¼ inches (2 by 26 cm).

7. Cut one inner pocket section from linen and one from interfacing, 12 by 8 inches (30 by 20 cm).

CONSTRUCTION

Seam allowances are ⅜ inch (1 cm) except as noted.

1. Following manufacturer's instructions, fuse interfacing to the wrong sides of pack front, back, and bottom; to the cargo pocket front and bottom pieces; and to one upper pocket and one flap section.

2. Fold the pack front piece in half lengthwise and round the upper corners (on the model, the upper corners are rounded more than the lower corners). Use a cup or bowl as a template. Use the front piece to round the back corners in the same way.

3. Make the inner pocket. With right sides together, center the zipper along one short edge and stitch along the zipper tape stitching line. Stitch the other end to the other side of the zipper in the same way. Open the zipper part way. With the piece wrong side out, fold it so that the zipper is approximately 1 inch (2.5 cm) below the upper fold. Stitch the sides; trim and turn.

4. Center the pocket on the wrong side of the pack back, the upper edge approximately 4 inches (10 cm) below the pack upper edge. Baste. From the right side, topstitch the pocket in place with a double row of stitching between the zipper and the pocket upper edge.

5. Make the cargo pocket. Fold the pocket front in half and slightly round the upper and lower corners as for the pack sections. Neaten and overlap the tape ends at the tops of two 9-inch (23-cm) zippers and zigzag them together so the zippers are joined head to head. Fold each zipper gusset piece in half lengthwise, right side out, and press. Stitch a strip onto the right side of each zipper tape, the fold along the zipper tape stitching line. Stitch close to the fold, then again near the edge of the zipper tape.

6. Fold under and press the seam allowance at one short end of each pocket bottom piece. Place a piece with the folded end across the bottom of each zipper, and stitch with a double row of stitching. Pin the front piece to the zipper strip with right sides together, beginning by placing the center of the top front at the zipper join. Pin to a point approximately 2 inches (5 cm) past each lower corner. Stitch the pinned area. Pin the remaining ends of the bottom section with right sides together, matching the length to the pocket front. Stitch and trim. Finish the front/bottom seam. Trim the seam allowances to a scant $\frac{1}{4}$ inch (.5 cm) and press open.

7. With the pocket right side out, crease and press along the seam. Stitch again, as for an inside-out French seam, slightly more than $\frac{1}{4}$ inch (.7 cm) from the folded edge, encasing the seam allowances.

8. To position the pocket on the bag, place it finished side against the bag front, centering it approximately $2\frac{1}{2}$ inches (6.5 cm) above the lower edge, and chalk mark the outline. Now turn it right side up and, with the zipper open, pin the remaining zipper gusset edge

to the bag, right sides together, following the outline. Stitch, and press from the right side. Trim the seam allowance. Topstitch the pocket in place, stitching on the zipper gusset $\frac{1}{4}$ inch (.7 cm) from the seam, encasing the raw edges as before. Break the stitching at the corners if necessary to avoid stitching pleats.

9. Make the upper pocket. Stitch the two pocket sections, right sides together, leaving an opening for turning. Trim, turn, and press. Center the pocket on the bag front, the lower edge approximately $\frac{3}{4}$ inch (2 cm) above the upper edge of the cargo pocket. Edgestitch in place along the sides and bottom, stitching a triangle at each upper corner for reinforcement.

10. Stitch the flap sections with right sides together, leaving one long edge open. Trim; turn. Topstitch around the finished edges, and baste the raw edges together. Center the flap over the pocket, the unfinished upper edge approximately $1\frac{1}{4}$ inches (3 cm) above the pocket top. Position the leather strip over the flap upper edge and edgestitch it in place, securing the flap. Sew a snap to the underside of each flap lower corner, and in the corresponding position on the pocket.

11. Make the back straps. For the lower attachment loops, cut two pieces of webbing 4 inches (10 cm) long. Fold each through the lower loop of a slide and baste the ends together to the lower edge of the back, approximately $1\frac{1}{2}$ inches (4 cm) in from the corners.

12. Stitch each of the long strap sections to a webbing piece along the long edges, right sides together, with $\frac{1}{4}$ inch (.5 cm) seam allowance, leaving about 1 inch (2.5 cm) unsewn at one end. Turn right side out (a large safety pin is helpful for this). Fold the unsewn end, back to front, over the center bar of one remaining slide. Fold under the end neatly and stitch to the strap, stitching close to the bar. Pull the other strap end through the upper loop of the slide on the attachment loop, then through the slide just sewn in place. (See the drawing on page 38.)

13. Make the handle. Stitch the linen to the webbing as for the straps (the handle will be wider) and turn right side out. Fold the piece in half to form a point.

Pin to the upper bag back, right side (webbing side) down, with the handle ends downward and placed evenly, side by side, about 2¼ inches (6 cm) from the bag upper edge. Position the strap ends, right side down, outside the handle ends, all edges even. Baste.

14. Place one leather reinforcement piece over the strap ends on the outside of the bag, above the pocket stitching. Glue baste. Position the other reinforcement piece in the same position inside the back. Push a pin through at each corner to aid in placement. Glue baste. From the outside, edgestitch the pieces in place, then stitch again about ¼ inch (.5 cm) inside the first stitching. Stitch an X from corner to corner.

15. Make the zipper gusset. Fold the gusset pieces in half lengthwise, right side out, as for the cargo pocket. Mark the center of each. Join the two long zippers at the upper ends as before. Stitch one fabric section to one zipper tape, placing the center of the strip at the zipper join and stitching close to the folded edge. Stitch again near the edge of the zipper tape. Stitch the other strip in the same way. Stitch one end of the bottom section to one end of the zipper gusset with right sides together.

16. Mark the top center of the pack front and back pieces. Starting at the unsewn end of the zipper gusset, pin it to the back with right sides together, matching upper centers. Stitch to just around the second

lower corner. Stitch the front in place in the same way. Carefully match the free end of the bottom to the front and back seamlines. Trim as necessary and fold under the end to align with the seamline at the end of the gusset. Topstitch to the gusset. Finish stitching the front and back seams. Trim, press, and re-stitch the seams as described in step 7.

Two large pockets outside and another inside keep everything in good order. Black accents—the topstitching, zippers, and synthetic leather trim—are a nice contrast to the neutral fabric color.

Almost Bottomless Backpack

Instructions begin on page 21
Enlarge all pieces 210%

Almost Bottomless Backpack
PACK TOP

Almost Bottomless Backpack
PACK FRONT FLAP

placement for hook & loop tape

placement for security strap carriers

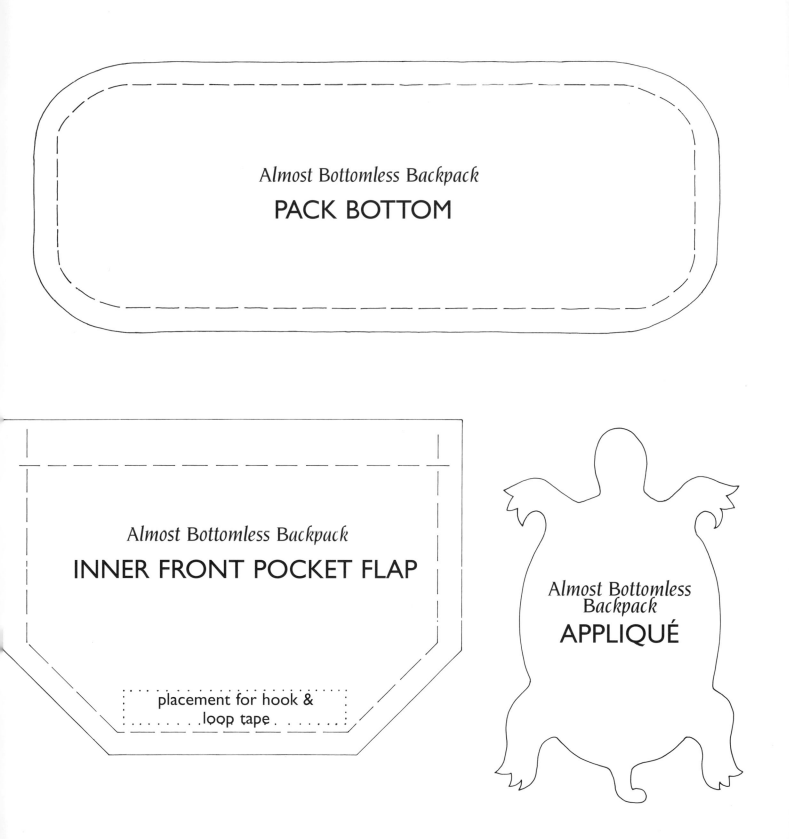

Almost Bottomless Backpack

PACK BOTTOM

Almost Bottomless Backpack

INNER FRONT POCKET FLAP

placement for hook &
loop tape.

*Almost Bottomless
Backpack*

APPLIQUÉ

City Pack

Instructions begin on page 37. Enlarge the pattern pieces 225%

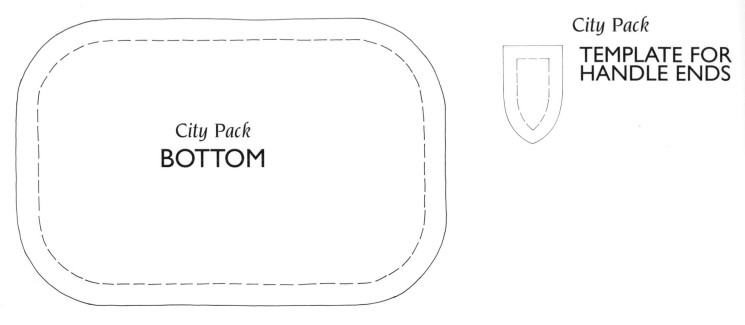

City Pack
BOTTOM

City Pack

TEMPLATE FOR HANDLE ENDS

Hemp Rucksack

Instructions begin on page 29. Enlarge the pattern pieces 250%

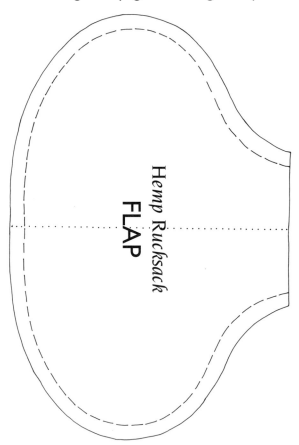

Hemp Rucksack
FLAP

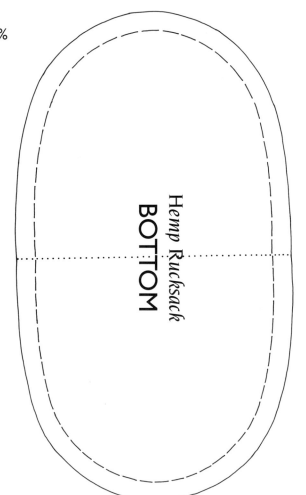

Hemp Rucksack
BOTTOM

Carryall Variations

The classic carryall is a wonderful thing. It can be pressed into service for all sorts of chores, then tossed onto the closet shelf until it's needed again.

On the following pages are some unusual carryalls that work every bit as well as the ho-hum canvas types, but are a great deal more fun to carry, and certainly more interesting to make! Duplicate the designs as they are shown, or just use them to inspire your own creative ideas.

An almost-classic leather carryall features a few very original details. **Design: Pat Scheible**

Carriage Bag

At first glance it's a classic tote made of beautiful, supple cowhide. But closer inspection reveals that the straps are backed with sports zippers and attached to the bag with animal-eye grommets!

The unlined bag is larger at the top for easy access to the contents. A side/bottom gusset creates neatly rounded lower corners. Inside, large pockets are sewn into the hem at the bag upper edge. The bag is 9½ inches (24 cm) wide, 14 inches (35.5 cm) high, and 5 inches (12.5 cm) deep at the center.

If you prefer a more traditional rendition of the design, use 1¼-inch (3-cm) grosgrain ribbon to face the straps, and attach the straps with ⅜-inch (1-cm) grommets or backed buttons. The bag might also be made of synthetic leather or suede.

SUPPLIES

- Leather: enlarge the pattern and take it with you to buy the skin. Use the zippers to measure for the straps. For synthetic leather, you will need ¾ yard (.7 m).
- Two sports zippers, 28-inch (71-cm) length, or two pieces of 1¼-inch (3-cm) grosgrain ribbon this length
- Eight animal eyes or grommets: ⅜ inch (1 cm) diameter
- Pocket fabric: ⅜ yard (.35 m)
- Permanent contact cement
- Wood or rubber mallet

CUTTING

1. Enlarge the pattern pieces on pages 63 and 64 and cut from paper.

2. For the bag, cut two each of the front/back and the side/bottom gusset.

3. Trim ½ inch (1.5 cm) off each end of the zipper tapes, then cut two straps the same length and width.

4. For pocket backs, cut two rectangles 11½ by 8¾ inches (29 by 22 cm). For the fronts, cut two rectangles 9½ by 8¾ inches (24 by 22 cm).

CONSTRUCTION

Please read the tips on sewing with leather, page 6. Seam allowance is ⅜ inch except as noted.

1. Make the pockets. Hem one short end of each pocket front section with a ⅜-inch (1-cm) double hem. Sew the sections together with French seams. Place a pocket front and back with *wrong* sides together, raw edges aligned. Stitch with ¼ inch (.5 cm) seam allowance. Trim away half the seam allowance. Turn wrong side out and press along the seamline. Stitch again, right sides together, encasing the seam allowances. Clip the pocket back seam allowances at the upper edge of the pocket front. Fold double, and stitch.

2. Stitch the short ends of the bag side/bottom gusset pieces with right sides together. Tap the seamline with a mallet, then glue the seam allowances open.

3. Stitch a back/front section to each side of the gusset. Tap and glue the seam allowances as before.

4. Center a pocket on the front and the back, the pocket upper edges 1¼ inches (3 cm) below the bag upper edge. Glue baste.

5. Fold and press a 1¼-inch (3-cm) hem around the top of the bag. Glue, then stitch close to the hem raw edge, catching the pockets in the stitching.

6. Make the straps. With wrong sides together, stitch a zipper (or ribbon) to each leather strip. If ribbon is used, zigzag the ends or apply fray retardant before stitching.

7. Position the handles with the ends just below the hem stitching line and centered over the seamlines. Fasten in place with the eyes or grommets.

A needlepoint sampler fetches more compliments as a carryall than as a wall hanging. **Design: Nell Paulk**

Bargello Carryall

A practical carryall is the perfect way to show off a beautiful piece of needlework, and needlepoint worked in Persian yarn makes a very durable bag. This one is trimmed with sturdy handwoven cotton and lined with heavy cotton as well.

A bag like this one makes a good beginner's needlepoint project. For experienced stitchers, it provides a good excuse to play with new stitches and color combinations. Copy the designs shown, or refer to needlepoint books for design ideas.

The finished bag is 13 inches (33 cm) wide, 11 inches (28 cm) high, and 4 inches (10 cm) deep.

SUPPLIES

- Bargello canvas, 13 count: 15 by 29 inches (38 by 73.5 cm)
- Persian yarn in assorted colors
- Fabric for strap, band, and gusset: ⅝ yard (.6 m), 40 inches (102 cm) or wider
- Lining fabric: ⅜ yard (.35 m)

CUTTING

1. Cut two side gusset pieces, 5 by 11½ inches (12.5 by 29 cm).

2. Cut one strap, 8 by 40 inches (20 by 102 cm).

3. Cut one edge band, 5 by 35 inches (12.5 by 89 cm).

4. Cut one piece for lining, 18 by 25 inches (45.5 by 63.5 cm).

CONSTRUCTION

Seam allowance is ½ inch (1.5 cm) except as noted.

1. Work the needlepoint, leaving 1-inch (2.5-cm) borders at the sides of the canvas and 2 inches (5 cm) top and bottom. Steam the piece to square it, and let it dry. Trim the side margins to ½ inch (1.5 cm).

2. With right sides together, stitch one long edge of the canvas to the long edges and one end of a gusset strip. Sew the second gusset strip to the other side of the canvas. Overcast the seam allowances.

3. Make the lining. Fold the piece in half crosswise, right sides together. Stitch the sides. To box the lower corners, fold a point at the lower end of each seam. Stitch across the point, perpendicular to the seam, approximately 2½ inches (6.5 cm) from the end of the seam (refer to the drawing on page 12). Trim.

4. With wrong sides together, place the lining in the bag. Baste together around the upper edges.

5. Make the strap. Fold the piece in half, lengthwise, with right sides together. Stitch with ¼ inch (.5 cm) seam allowance along the long edge. Turn and press. If desired, topstitch along both edges. Position the strap ends at the top of the side gussets, raw edges aligned. Baste.

6. Join the ends of the binding strip, right sides together, to form a circle. Press under the seam allowance on both long edges. Fold the piece evenly over the bag upper edge. Topstitch in place close to the lower edge. Fold the strap upward at the ends and stitch an X or a square to attach it to the binding.

The bag couldn't be easier to assemble, but an offbeat ornament makes it unique. **Design: Pat Scheible**

Tasseled Tote

A huge shiny tassel accents a very simple totebag design. Any special ornament would work just as well, but it might be fun to make just one huge tassel.

The bag is synthetic leather, lined with polyester satin. It would be beautiful in synthetic suede, too, or in the real thing. It measures 15 inches (38 cm) in height, and is 15 (38 cm) inches across the top.

SUPPLIES

- Fabric for outer bag: ⅝ yard (.6 m)
- Lining: ½ yard (.5 m)
- Tassel or other ornament
- Permanent contact cement

CUTTING

1. Cut two pieces for the bag front and back, 15¾ inches (40 cm) wide and 22⅜ inches (57 cm) long.

2. Cut one piece for the strap, 30 by 1½ inches (76 by 4 cm). 3. Cut two lining pieces, 21⅜ by 15¾ inches (54.5 by 40 cm).

3. For the ornament loop, cut a rectangle 3 by 1½ inches (7.5 by 4 cm).

CONSTRUCTION

Seam allowance is ⅜ inch (1 cm) except as noted.

1. Make the ornament loop. Fold the strip in half, lengthwise, right side out. Glue together at the center, keeping the ends flat. When the glue is dry trim the center portion slightly. Position the piece on the bag front. Stitch the loop ends to the bag.

2. Stitch the bag front to the back with right sides together. Press seams open. To box the lower corners, fold a point at the lower end of each side seam as shown in the drawing on page 12. Stitch across the point, perpendicular to the seam, approximately 6 inches (15 cm) from the end of the seam.

3. Stitch the lining sections with right sides together, leaving a long opening on the bottom for turning. Box the lower corners.

4. Place the bag inside the lining, right sides together, matching the upper edges. Stitch around the upper edge. Fit the lining well into the bottom of the bag. Fold and press the upper edge of the bag. Topstitch if desired.

A small loop on the front of the bag allows you to change the ornament to suit the occasion—or your mood.

Walker Carryall

Anyone who has ever used a walker, even temporarily, can appreciate the usefulness of this specially designed tote. With both hands on the walker it's difficult to carry anything.

This one is made of lightweight Cordura, a tough fabric that is easy to keep clean. The outer pockets are decorated with colorful stitching and with patchwork strips of the nylon in an assortment of bright colors. Clear vinyl pockets display photos of friends and relatives.

Instructions are for the larger bag shown. It is 10 inches (25.5 cm) wide, 12 inches (30.5 cm) high, and 1¾ inches (4.5 cm) deep. To make a smaller version, shorten the length of the main and pocket pieces, and shorten the side gussets by half that amount.

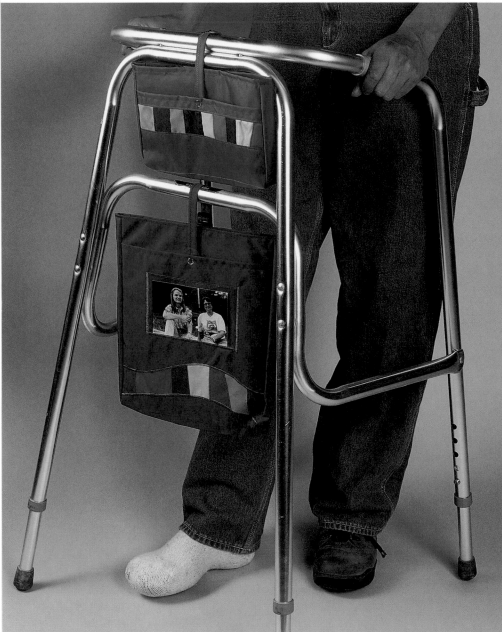

SUPPLIES

- Nylon fabric: ¾ yard (.7 m)
- Fast X buckle, ¾ inch (2 cm) width
- Two large snaps
- Assorted scraps for appliqué, if desired
- Clear vinyl for photo pockets

CUTTING

1. Cut one main bag piece, 26½ by 11 inches (67.5 by 28 cm).

2. Cut one outer pocket section, 23½ by 11 inches (60 by 28 cm).

3. Cut two side gussets, 2½ by 13 inches (6.5 by 33 cm).

4. Cut one strap, 1¾ by 15 inches (4.5 by 38 cm).

5. Cut vinyl rectangles for photo pockets, allowing slight ease beyond the photo measurements.

Carryalls that buckle over the walker frame are extremely useful. **Design: Margaret Gregg**

CONSTRUCTION

Seam allowance is ½ (1.5 cm) inch except as noted.

1. Hem both short ends of the outer pocket with ½ inch (1 cm) single hems. For fabric other than non-raveling nylon, clean finish the edges before hemming.

2. Fold the strap in thirds, right side out, and zigzag to cover the raw edge. Cut off a 4-inch (10-cm) piece. Clean finish all ends.

3. Decorate the pocket. Use appliqué or just decorative stitching. Finish the upper edges of the photo pockets with a zigzag stitch and decorative thread. Attach them to the pocket in the same way.

4. Attach the snaps and buckle. A 1-inch (2.5-cm) circle of vinyl between the pocket side of the snap and the pocket will make the snap easier to open. Attach one snap section with knob to the inner hemmed edge at the pocket center front on each end. Attach one corresponding snap section 1½ inches (4 cm) from one end of the longer strap piece. Slip the shorter strap through the lower buckle. Attach the remaining snap through both layers, approximately 1¼ inches (3 cm) below the buckle. Loop the free end of the longer strap through the upper buckle section and stitch through both layers.

5. Center the pocket on the main bag section, both pieces right side up. Baste along the sides. Mark the bag bottom: fold the piece in half crosswise and crease the fold. Chalk a line ¾ inch (2 cm) to either side of the crease to designate the bottom.

6. Join the side gussets to the main section. With right sides together, stitch the bottom first, then the front and back.

7. Fold and stitch a ½-inch (1-cm) single hem around the upper edge.

A totebag made up of pieced linen samplers is nothing short of fabulous. **Design: dj Bennett**

Linen Samplers

This beautifully designed bag exhibits a wealth of fabrics and textures. Dozens of techniques, worked on assorted natural linen scraps, were pieced to create an exquisite patchwork that is also a very useful car-ryall. The back is a single piece of cotton sateen, machine quilted to thin batting for a different textural effect.

The strap, too, is made up of small samplers. Connect-ing each strap to the bag is the appropriate sewer's trademark: an empty thread spool.

SUPPLIES

- See cutting instructions, below, for the measurements of each bag section
- Assorted fabric scraps to piece for the bag front and strap (see cutting dimensions, below)for the bag back
- Garment-weight batting, for the bag back
- Lining fabric
- Fabric strip for the strap facing and small pieces for the strap connectors
- Fusible interfacing, for the strap facing
- Bias fabric strip for piping, 42 by 1½ inches (107 by 4 cm)
- Piping cord: 42 inches (107 cm), ¼ inch (.7 cm) diameter
- Two thread spools

CUTTING

1. For the bag front, join the small samplers to create a single piece 12 inches (31 cm) wide and 15 inches (38.5 cm) long.

2. Cut batting and bag back fabric slightly larger than the front piece, then trim to the size of the front after quilting.

3. Cut the strap facing 36 by 2½ inches (91 by 6.5 cm). Cut interfacing this size. Piece small samplers to this size for the outer strap.

4. For strap connectors, cut two pieces 15 by 1 ¼

inches (38 by 3 cm). Cut four pieces 5 to 6 inches (12.5 to 15 cm) long, depending upon the diameter of your spools. The width should be equal to the length of the central portion of the spools.

5. Cut two lining pieces, 16 by 13 inches (41 by 33 cm).

DECORATING

1. Make samplers for the bag front and strap, experi-menting with as many different techniques as you can imagine. Our model includes tucks, folded pleats, machine embroidery, cutwork, quilting, and double needle pintucks. Plan the fabrics and thread colors for the best overall effect.

2. Quilt the back. Use batting to give dimension to the design. Plan a stitched design that complements or repeats some of the elements of the front (see the photo on page 62). Trim to size after quilting.

CONSTRUCTION

Seam allowance is ½ inch (1.5 cm) except as noted.

1. Make the piping. Wrap the bias, right side out, around the piping cord. Stitch close to the cord with a zipper or piping foot. Pin the piping to the right side of the bag front, raw edges outward and the piping stitch-ing line on the bag seamline. Round the lower corners slightly, and clip into the piping seam allowance around the corners for a smooth fit. Stitch just next to the piping stitching line.

2. Join the bag back to the front, right sides together, stitching on the previous stitching line. Trim the cor-ners; turn.

3. Stitch the lining sections, right sides together, along the sides and lower edge. Trim, turn, and press. Put the lining in the bag, wrong sides together. Pin together along the bottom seams. At the upper edge, fold the lining over the bag upper edge. Press the fold.

The back of the bag features an elaborate quilted design that is backed with lightweight batting to give it dimension.

Turn under the raw edge to create a band approximately ¾ inch (2 cm) wide. Stitch close to the lower edge.

4. Make the strap connectors. Fold each of the longer strips in half lengthwise, right side out, and press. Fold the long raw edges in to the center, press, and stitch along both long edges.

5. Put the shorter connectors together in pairs, right sides out. Work satin stitch all the way around the edge of each pair. Fold each strip in half around a spool, and stitch across close to the spool.

6. Make the strap. Fuse interfacing to the strap facing. Place the facing and strap with wrong sides together. Cut a point at the 2 inches (5 cm) of each strap end. Then cut off the point so the end is the same width as the strap connector on the spool. Sandwich the strap connector ends between the strap and facing at each end; stitch close to the strap end. Work satin stitch along both long edges and across the ends, stitching the connectors in place.

7. Slip a long connector strip through the spindle hole in each spool. Pin the ends into the bag approximately 5 inches (12 cm), placing them together along the side seamlines. From the right side, stitch them in place, stitching in the ditch of the side seams. Stitch across at the base of the upper band.

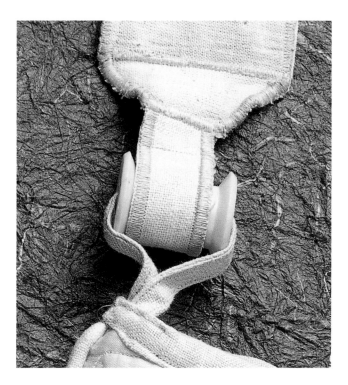

Carriage Bag

Instructions are on page 51
Enlarge this pattern piece and the side/bottom gusset piece, page 64, 210%

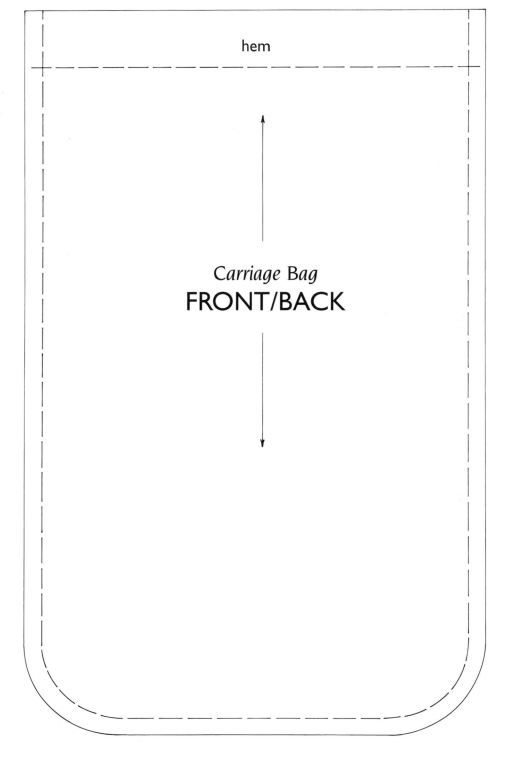

hem

Carriage Bag
FRONT/BACK

Carriage Bag

See page 63 for size information

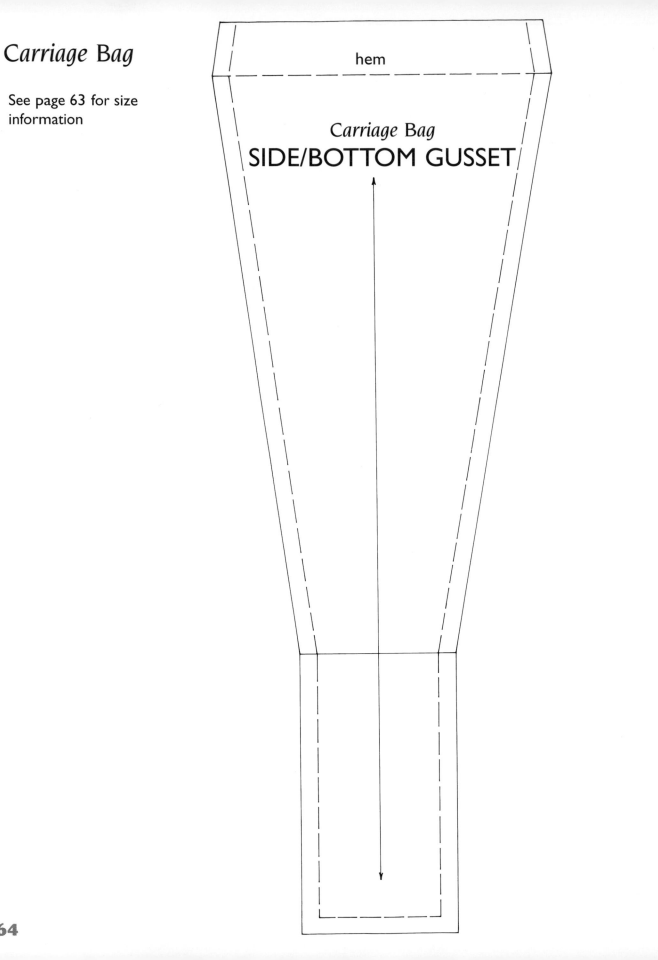

hem

Carriage Bag
SIDE/BOTTOM GUSSET

Shopping & Other Expeditions

Whether it's a short trip from the market or an extended transoceanic voyage, it seems there is always something to be carried along. The bags shown in this chapter offer lots of options: there are compact types that fold up to be carried in a purse until their services are needed, and there are bags that expand to accommodate an ever-increasing load.

When extra carrying capacity is needed, the sides of the bag can be unfastened to provide for just about anything you care to take along.
Design: Elma Johnson

Expandable Shoulder Bag

A very adaptable design, this travel bag presents a slim appearance when the sides are snapped together, then expands to hold a day's shopping or an extra layer of clothing. The straps are long enough to permit wearing the bag across the body for security, and the buckles allow adjustment to standard shoulder length. The large front pocket has an additional zippered pocket hidden on the underside of the flap. The bag offers plenty of pocket options. It would be a simple matter to add an open patch pocket on the back and one or two more on the lining.

Finished size is 14½ inches (37 cm) wide at center, 15½ inches (39.5 cm) high. Closed, it is approximately 2 inches (5 cm) deep; it opens to an accommodating depth of 7½ inches (19 cm).

The designer chose natural canvas for the model so the construction details would be visible. The lining is tightly woven cotton. Nearly any sturdy fabric would work well for this design—linen, leather, tapestry, denim, slipcover-weight cotton and cotton velvet, to suggest just a few. Keep in mind that you will be sewing through multiple layers of fabric and choose material that your machine can handle. If the fabric thickness results in skipped stitches, try a heavier needle with a coating and/or a sharp point.

SUPPLIES

- Fabric for outer bag: 1 yard (1 m), 45 to 60 inches (115 to 152 cm) wide
- Lining: 1 yard (1 m), any width
- Two buckles: 1¼ inches (3.2 cm) wide
- Two rectangular attachment rings: 1¼ inches (3.2 cm) wide
- Zipper, for pocket flap: 6 inches (15 cm), or remove teeth from the upper end of a 7-inch (17.5-cm) zipper after stitching it in place.
- Two large snaps or small hook and loop tape buttons
- Optional: Metal eyelets for the straps

CUTTING

1. Enlarge the pattern pieces on page 80 and cut from paper.

2. With the pattern, cut one front/back on the fabric crossgrain fold. Cut two sides. Transfer markings.

3. Cut one pocket back/flap piece, 8 inches (20 cm) wide and 15¼ inches (38.5 cm) long. For the flap facing, cut one piece 8 inches (20 cm) wide and 7½ inches (19 cm) long. Cut one pocket front, 8 inches (20 cm) wide and 10¾ inches (27 cm) long.

4. Cut all strap pieces 4 inches (10 cm) wide. Cut two straps, 46 inches (117 cm) long. Cut four strap extensions, 7½ inches (19 cm) long.

5. Cut lining from the bag pattern pieces: one front/back and two sides. Cut pocket(s) for lining, if desired.

CONSTRUCTION

Seam allowance is ⅝ inch (1.5 cm) except where noted. If you plan to include additional pockets on the bag or lining, apply them before assembling the bag or lining.

1. Stitch the darts in the bag front and back. Slit the seam allowance almost to the point and press open. Stitch darts in the side sections: Fold each piece in half lengthwise, wrong side out. On the crease, mark a point 1¼ inches (3 cm) below the upper edge and another 5½ inches (14 cm) below the first. Stitch the narrowest possible dart along the crease between the two points.

2. Make the pocket. With a template, round the corners slightly on the upper and lower edges of the pocket back/flap, the upper edge of the flap facing, and the lower edge of the pocket front.

3. Cut a 3-inch (7.5-cm) strip from the lower (straight) edge of the flap facing. Clean finish the cut edge of each piece. With right sides together, center the zipper along the finished edge of one piece to one side of the zipper, matching edges. Stitch on the marked line on the zipper tape. Stitch the finished edge of the other flap piece to the other zipper tape in the same way. Press. Stitch across the ends on the side seamlines.

4. Hem the upper edge of the pocket front. Fold 1⅝ inches (4 cm) to the wrong side; press. Fold under the raw edge ⅜ inch (1 cm); press. Stitch close to the fold. With right sides together and matching the lower corners, stitch the pocket front to the pocket back/flap. Trim close to the stitching.

5. With right sides together and upper corners matched, stitch the flap facing to the pocket back/flap, ending the stitching at the upper edge of the pocket front. Trim seam allowances and turn to the right side. At the flap lower edge, fold under the edge so that the fold extends approximately ½ inch (1.5 cm) below the upper edge of the pocket front. Press. Trim the side seam allowances as necessary. Stitch close to the fold. Edgestitch the flap.

6. Center the pocket on the bag front with the pocket flap closed, the upper edge of the pocket 2¼ inches (5.5 cm) below the bag upper edge. Pin. Topstitch the pocket in place, matching the stitching on the flap, and stitch across the lower end of the flap just above the upper edge of the pocket front.

7. Assemble the bag. With right sides together, stitch a side piece between each front/back section, matching notches and clipping at corners as necessary. Reinforce at the lower corners and across the bottom of each side with a second row of stitching close to the first in the seam allowance. Trim the seam allowances to a scant ¼ inch (.5 cm). Press open. Press under the ¾-inch (2-cm) hem allowance at the upper edge of the bag, but do not stitch.

8. Make the straps. Fold each strap section in half lengthwise; press. On the long straps, press under the seam allowance at one end. On the long edges of all straps, press the seam allowances toward the wrong side. Note: with some fabrics it is helpful to first stitch along the seamline, then fold and press. Stitch close to the

long edges of each piece, and across the pressed ends of the long straps. Overcast one short end of each shorter strap and the two unfinished ends of the longer straps.

9. On two of the shorter strap sections, punch a hole for the buckle prong 4 inches (10 cm) from the unfinished end. Slip the finished strap end through the buckle bar and the prong through the hole. Fold under the overcast strap end and stitch a rectangle to secure it to the strap. Attach the rings to the remaining two short straps. Double and stitch the overcast ends as for the buckle straps.

10. On the longer straps, attach eyelets or punch holes for length adjustment. Position the first one approximately 5 inches (12.5 cm) from the finished end, then space another five or six approximately 2 inches (5 cm) apart, or as desired.

11. Attach the overcast end of each strap to the remaining side of a ring, stitching as for the lower strap. Buckle the straps.

12. Position the lower (shorter) strap sections on the bag with right sides together. With the front of the bag facing you, place the strap section on the ring at the right side of the bag, the strap inner edge just outside the dart seam and the unfinished end even with the bag upper edge. Position the short strap section with the buckle at the left side of the front in the same way, its inner edge just outside the dart seam. Turn the bag over and pin the other strap in the same way. Make sure the straps are not twisted. Stitch the strap ends securely to the bag hem allowance (¾ inch or 2 cm). Stitch a rectangle, then an X within it for reinforcement.

13. Make the lining. Stitch the lining sides to the front/back as for the outer bag. Trim and overcast the seam allowances.

14. With right sides together, place the bag inside the lining. Arrange the straps between the bag and lining so they lie between the darts at front and back, out of the way. With upper edges even, pin the lining to the bag, leaving open between the front darts. Stitch with

⅜ inch (1.5 cm) seam allowance. Turn right side out through the opening. Press under the lining seam allowance and stitch the lining in place by hand. Press.

15. Add the finishing touches. Topstitch around the upper edge, barely catching the lining in the stitching. Crease the side/front and side/back seams along the seamlines. Keeping the lining free, topstitch each

seam, stitching from near the bottom of the bag and as close as possible to the upper edge.

16. Sew snaps or hook and loop tape buttons at each side. To mark the positions, fold the seams together at each side and use a pin to mark a spot approximately ¾ inch (2 cm) below the bag upper edge and the same distance in from the side seam.

When it is closed at the sides, the bag presents a trim profile but still is quite roomy.

The groceries seem more appetizing when they are carried home in an attractive net shopping bag. **Design: Marilyn Hastings**

Crocheted Shopper

With the net bag tucked up inside, it's a pretty cabbage rose just 4 inches (10 cm) in diameter, convenient to keep at hand in the glove compartment so it's always ready for a stop at the grocery store. It expands gracefully to hold a surprising amount.

The outer rose is crocheted with standard weight crochet cotton. The inner net bag can be worked with the same thread or a finer weight. We have used two colors for contrast.

SUPPLIES

- Mercerized crochet cotton, size 10 (a finer thread can be used for the net bag if desired)
- Crochet hook: U.S. size 0

INSTRUCTIONS

The Cabbage Rose

Ch 8, join with sl st to first ch to form a ring.

Rnd 1: Ch 1 (counts as 1 sc), work 15 sc into ring, join with sl st (16 sc).

CROCHET ABBREVIATIONS

ch	chain
dc	double crochet
hdc	half double crochet
rep	repeat
rnd	round
sc	single crochet
sl st	slip stitch
tr	treble (triple) crochet
* *	repeat the steps between asterisks the number of times indicated

Rnd 2: *Ch 5, skip 1 sc, sc into next sc, rep from * around (8 loops).

Rnd 3: Into each loop work 1 sc, 1 hdc, 5 dc, 1 hdc, 1 sc. Join with sl st (8 petals).

Rnd 4: Ch 3 (to move to the center of the 1st petal), sc around the middle dc of the petal from the back (this rather unconventional move gives depth to the petal), ch 6, *sc around middle dc of next petal, ch 6.* Rep from * around (8 loops offset behind first round of petals).

Rnd 5: Into each loop, work 1 sc, 1 hdc, 3 dc, 3 tr, 3 dc, 1 hdc, 1 sc. Join with sl st (8 petals).

Rnd 6: Ch 5 (to move to the center of the 1st petal), sc around the middle tr of the petal from the back, ch 9, *sc around middle tr of next petal, ch 9.* Rep from * around (8 loops offset behind second round of petals).

Rnd 7: Into each loop, work 1 sc, 1 hdc, 4 dc, 3 tr, 4 dc, 1 hdc, 1 sc. Join with sl st (8 petals).

The bag stores neatly in an attached cabbage rose case that is just 4 inches (10 cm) in diameter.

71

Rnd 8: From back side between every other loop made in rnd 7 sc onto the loops made in rnd 6.

Make two cabbage roses.

Join the two roses together (right sides out) by sc though the sc of rnd 8 on both roses for 5 petals, and through each rose separately for the last 3 petals (for opening).

String Bag

Turn the joined cabbage roses inside out.

Rnd 1: Join the new thread by sc to one of the joining sc, *ch 6, skip one sc, and sc into the next sc.* Rep around, join using a sl st.

Rnd 2 and remaining rnds: Ch 3, sc into 1st loop, *ch 8, sc into loop.* Rep from * until bag is 12 inches deep

To begin the bag itself, stitches are worked around the inside of one of the rose sections.

(working in a spiral rather than joining each round). Join the last round with a sl st.

Top: 6 sc into each loop. Work 4 rnds of sc for top band.

Handles: Divide length of top band into quarters, 48 sc in each.

For 1st handle, ch 75, join at beginning of 2nd 4th, sc into next sc of top band, ch 1, turn, sc into 2nd ch stitch, sc into all ch across, sc into sc of top band, ch 1, *(turn, sc across handle again, sc into sc of top band, ch 1, turn,* 4 more times, but the last time continue sc across top band (without ch 1 and turn) to the beginning of the 3rd quarter. Start 2nd handle by ch 75 and continue as 1st handle. Then continue sc across top band, over 1st handle again, across top band on the other side, finally across 2nd handle, and fasten off thread after reaching top band again. (This last round adds strength and unity to the handles.)

Closure/wrist strap: Attach rose thread in middle of center petal of opening; ch 11 inches; attach to opposite middle petal, and lock thread. Pull loop through first center petal to close bag. Loop can be worn over the wrist, or tied to keep closed and moved to the side to take bag out of the cabbage rose case.

Weave in all loose threads and cut them off.

Crocheted Net Rucksack

The crocheted rucksack looks delicate, but has a huge capacity.
Design: Amy Mozingo

Made to be slung over the shoulder rucksack style, this bag seems to have an unlimited capacity. The handles slip through D-rings to close the top securely. In its relaxed state the bag is approximately 12 inches (30 cm) high and 15 inches (38 cm) wide.

The yarn used to make the model is a blend of cotton, rayon, and silk. Choose a reasonably sturdy yarn that can bear the load you will carry in the bag.

SUPPLIES

- Yarn or thread: Similar to 4-ply wool, approximately 300 yards (275 m)
- Crochet hook: U.S. size F
- Six metal D-rings, 1½ to 2 inches (4 to 5 cm) diameter

INSTRUCTIONS

For crochet abbreviations, see page 71.

Gauge: 5 sc equal 1 inch (2.5 cm); 4 rows sc equal 1 inch (2.5 cm).

Crochet a chain 7 stitches long. Sc in the 3rd ch from hook. Sc in each remaining ch, ch 2 (counts as 1st sc on next row), turn. Sc in each stitch, ch 2, turn. Repeat until crocheted strip is 4 to 5 inches (10 to 12.5 cm) long.

Fold strip in half and on the next row treat both ends as one. 1 sc through both stitches to end of row. Ch 2, sc in only 1 loop of the stitch on the previous row (the outside loop); at the end of the row place 2 sc in 1 loop to turn the corner and continue crocheting in the same stitches but in the loop not used the first time across. At the end, sc in the first sc of the last row. Now begin the upward spiral.

Rnd 1: 2 sc in each stitch (return to crocheting through both loops of each stitch) to 1st 2-sc pair.

Rnd 2: 2 sc in the middle of each 2-sc pair, and 1 sc in the stitch between.

Rnd 3 and subsequent rnds: 2 sc in the middle of each previous 2-sc pair and 1 sc in each stitch between.

When the circle (with the center loop) is approximately 5 inches (12.5 cm) in diameter: ch 3, 1 dc, ch 1 in each stitch until the circle is complete. Sl st together. Ch 5, 1 sc in ch 1 space on previous row. Repeat until there is a sc in the last possible ch 1 space. Ch 6, sc in the middle of the first ch loop. Do not crochet through the stitch, rather go around the entire ch 5 loop. This will make the bag stronger. Crochet as before and at the first ch 6 loop, begin to ch 7. Continue in this manner, adding another ch 1 to the loop until there are 9 ch in each loop. Then continue crocheting around the bag until the desired length of the bag is reached. In the bag illustrated there are 15 rounds with a 9-chain loop.

Final rnd: This row can be a bit tricky, but it isn't difficult. Here's what you're trying to achieve: 3 or 4 loops

will be gathered onto each ring, and as you crochet, the thread will have to travel through all the rings until you reach the end. Then you can cut the thread and pull it out.

Continue crocheting as before but this time before the sc, slip a ring over the ch. Sc, ch 9 (here's where it gets tricky), put the chain through the ring in the last loop. Then sc where appropriate. Repeat until 4 of the loops pass through the ring. After the sc that finishes the 4th loop, ch 3, sc in next loop and repeat with a new ring. If you end up with 2, 3 or 5 loops in the final ring, that's fine. If the thread tangles during this process, cut the thread after each ring is attached, pull it free, knot the ends together, then continue.

Strap
Make a chain approximately 2 yards (1.85 m) long. *Sc in 4th ch from hook, ch 1, skip next ch, sc in next ch,* repeat to end of chain, ch 3, turn. 1 sc in each ch 1 space to end of chain, ch 3, turn.

Repeat last row. End off.

Thread strap through the rings and then pass through the bottom loop. Knot the strap together.

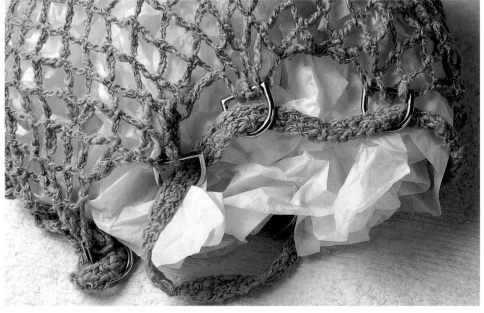
On the last round at the top of the bag, chains are worked through the D-rings to hold them in place.

Double-Duty Bag

his sturdy, practical bag goes together easily, and it offers unlimited options for custom embellishment. With the upper half folded down, it is a trim shoulder bag. Top up, it's a spacious tote with double the capacity.

This model is made of durable denim to withstand years of laundering and rough handling. The cheerful calico lining coordinates with the design around the bag opening.

With its top folded over, this shoulder bag serves as an everyday purse. **Design: Lori Kerr**

The bag itself can be assembled in an hour. Decorating it can take as much or as little time as you wish to invest. This one features a painted floral design highlighted with decorative stitching. On page 78 is a patchwork variation that is just as practical and completely different in appearance. Whatever medium you choose for the decoration, plan a design that "reads" the same right side up or upside down so it will look good whether the bag is open or closed.

The finished bag measures 16½ inches (42 cm) wide by 24 inches (61 cm) high. The strap is 53 inches (135 cm) long.

SUPPLIES

- Fabric for the bag and strap: ½ yard (.5 m)
- Lining fabric: ½ yard (.5 m)
- Optional, for embellishment:
- Fabric paints
- Decorative thread
- Tear-away backing or interfacing scrap

CUTTING

For a washable bag, preshrink the fabric by machine washing and drying it. Press the fabric in the direction of the lengthwise grain.

1. Cut two pieces for the bag front and back, 17½ inches (45 cm) wide by 25 inches (64 cm) long. Cut two lining pieces the same width and 1 inch (2.5 cm) shorter in length.

2. Cut one strap, 2¾ by 53 inches (6.5 by 135 cm). For narrower fabric widths, piece a strip to this length.

3. Cut one strap casing, 1¾ by 17½ inches (4.5 by 45 cm).

CONSTRUCTION

Seam allowance is ½ inch (1.5 cm) except as noted.

1. Decorate the upper edge of the bag front, keeping clear of the seam and 1-inch (2.5-cm) hem allowances.

For a combination of painting and stitching as shown here, paint a design and set the color according to the instructions with the paint. Back the area to be stitched with a tear-away backing or lightweight interfacing.

2. Fold the strap in half lengthwise, right sides together. Using ¼ inch (.5 cm) seam allowance, stitch the long edge. Turn and press. Topstitch the long edges if desired.

3. Make the strap casing. Press under 1 inch (2.5 cm) at each end, and press under the seam allowance on one long edge. Stitch across each end close to the fold and again near the raw edge. To position the casing, chalk a line across the bag front 10½ inches (26.5 cm) below the upper (decorated) edge. Center the casing on the bag front, right sides together, with the seamline of the unpressed edge along the marked line and the pressed edge toward the bag upper edge. Stitch along the seamline, backstitching securely at the ends.

4. Position the strap under the casing. Overlap the ends slightly at the center of the bag, folding a small pleat in each end so it will fit under the casing. Stitch the ends to each other and to the bag piece with a zigzag stitch. Fold the casing down over the strap and pin, keeping the strap free. Edgestitch in place. Press and edgestitch the upper edge.

5. Pin the bag front to the back, right sides together, keeping the strap free. Stitch the sides and bottom.

6. Stitch the lining sections as for the bag, but leave an opening of approximately 4 inches (10 cm) at the bottom for turning.

7. Place the bag in the lining, right sides together, and pin and stitch around the upper edge. Turn right side out through the lining opening. Stitch the opening, and pin the two together along the bottom seam. Smooth the two to establish the foldline at the upper edge of the bag. Press the fold, and topstitch if desired

With the top open, the bag becomes a good-sized carryall.

Patchwork Double-Duty Bag

Gaily colored cotton patchwork completely changes the character of the bag, but it is still every bit as practical. Fabric pieces are attached to a cotton backing by the flip piecing technique, then edges with machine embroidery stitches and an assortment of bright rayon threads.

Bright patchwork edged with decorative stitching gives the foldover bag a different character altogether. **Design: Lori Kerr**

SUPPLIES

- Fabric: Assorted scraps for the patchwork and strap. Backing fabric: muslin or similar cotton, ½ yard (.5 m)
- Lining fabric: ½ yard (.5 m)
- Decorative thread for embroidery

CUTTING

To prevent uneven shrinkage if you plan to wash the bag, wash and dry the fabrics before cutting to preshrink them.

Refer to cutting instructions on page 76 for sizes of the pieces. Cut backing fabric for the bag front and back, cutting slightly larger than the measurements given. Lightly mark the seamlines. These pieces will be trimmed to size after the patchwork is finished. Cut the strap and carrier the sizes given. Cut scraps for piecing; it is easiest to work with pieces that are square, or nearly so.

CONSTRUCTION

1. Attach the scraps to the backing. Beginning in an upper corner, position one fabric piece to cover the seamlines. Stitch in the seam allowance. Place a second piece, right sides together, along one of the inner edges of the first. Stitch the two together through the backing along one side using a narrow seam allowance. Flip the second piece right side out, and press. Continue placing pieces this way to cover the backing. If an edge of a piece will remain visible, fold under and press the seam allowance before stitching the adjacent edge.

2. When the backing is covered, baste around the outer edges. Work decorative stitching along the edges of each patchwork piece.

3. Construct the bag, following the steps on page 76. Try a decorative stitch to topstitch the strap edges and to sew the casing in place if you wish.

On this model, the strap and carrier are cut from single pieces of fabric. For more patchwork fun, they could be pieced onto backing fabric instead.

Expandable Shoulder Bag

Instructions begin
on page 67
Enlarge the pattern
pieces 315%

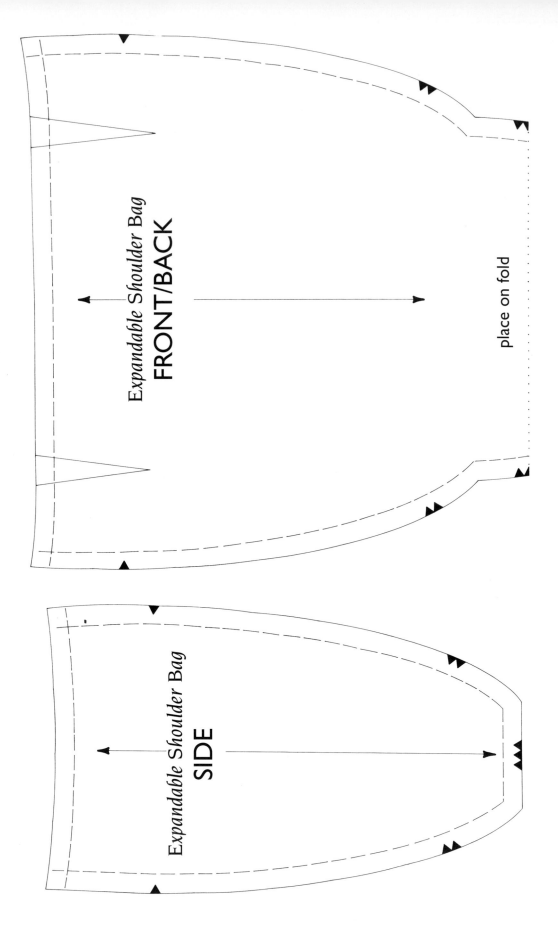

Expandable Shoulder Bag
FRONT/BACK

place on fold

Expandable Shoulder Bag
SIDE

Business on the Run

I t seems that wherever we go, our work goes with us—papers, folders, books, the laptop. Where a small, neat briefcase used to suffice, we now seem to need carryalls in a variety of shapes and sizes to accommodate our work. There is no reason to make do with an ancient, tattered totebag when there are so many beautiful alternatives! Take a weekend to make yourself a fabulous new "co-worker" from one of the designs shown on the following pages. Monday morning will be much brighter.

Two Totes in One

Two separate compartments make this an especially useful bag. Keep business papers in one side and your musical life—or personal items—in the other. The bag is easy to put together. It consists of a wide fabric tube, lined, folded in half, then stitched across the center to divide it in two. Made of a luxurious fabric like this wool and accented with some interesting details, it is a most attractive accessory.

On the model, extra pockets have been added to keep track of small items. An outside patch pocket protects the sunglasses. A tiny pocket for parking meter change attaches at the upper edge, extending to the front as a tab to show off a pretty pin. It wouldn't take much more time to add pockets to the lining while you're at it. Suggestions are on page 7.

Combine a simple design with great fabric for a very distinctive tote. Note that three of the strap ends are attached to the bag with connecting rings; the fourth is sewn at the bag edge and topped with a decorative pin. **Design: Lois Ericson**

There are plenty of possibilities for this bag. Sewn in denim with a water-repellant lining, it would be a useful carryall for baby gear. In sturdy, brightly colored cotton it is a great book bag for the students in the family.

SUPPLIES

- Fabric: tapestry, denim, or other sturdy fabric, 1 yard (.95 m)
- Lining: 1 yard (.95 m)
- Two large snaps
- Three rectangular rings, 1¼ inches (3 cm) wide
- For the key tab: a small swivel hook and one decorative button
- Ornament for bag front

CUTTING

1. For the bag main section, cut a rectangle of outer fabric and of lining, 28 by 36 inches (71 by 91 cm).

2. Cut a pocket section from fabric and from lining, 6 by 8 inches (15 by 20 cm).

3. For the handles, cut two strips 3 by 25 inches (7.5 by 63.5 cm), or desired length. Cut an additional strip the same width and 18 inches (46 cm) long for the strap attachment loops and key tab.

4. For the tab pocket, cut two pieces of fabric, 4 by 10 inches (10 by 25.5 cm).

CONSTRUCTION

Seam allowance is ½ inch (1.5 cm) except as noted.

1. Fold the main bag section in half lengthwise, right sides together, and stitch the long edges. Press seams open. Press a 1-inch (2.5-cm) hem at each end. Stitch and press the lining piece the same way.

2. Make the outer patch pocket. Trim a scant ⅛ inch (3mm) from the lining edges. Stitch lining and pocket, right sides together, leaving an opening at the bottom. Trim, turn, and press. Topstitch across the upper edge. Arrange the outer bag so that the seam will be to the inside when the bag is folded. Position the pocket on the outside front of the bag, approximately 3 inches (7.5 cm) below the upper edge. Topstitch in place, stitching a triangle at each upper corner for reinforcement.

3. Make the handles. Fold each strip in half lengthwise, right sides together, and stitch the long edge. Trim seam allowances and press open. Turn right side out. Center the seam, and press. At the ends, fold the seam allowances to the inside and press.

If fabric is too thick or stiff to turn, try this method. Press under the seam allowance on one long edge. Fold to a width of 1 inch (2.5 cm), the pressed edge

The bag is essentially a lined tube, open at both ends, stitched and folded at the center.

overlapping and close to the strap edge. Fold and press the ends under; topstitch the long edge.

4. For the strap attachment loops, stitch the remaining strip as for the handles, but leave the ends unfinished. Cut three lengths, 3¼ inches (8 cm) long. Finish one end of the remaining piece to use for the key tab.

5. Make the change pocket. Make a bound buttonhole in one pocket section. Cut a lining scrap approximately 1½ by 3½ inches (4 by 9 cm). Chalk a line 2½ inches (6.5 cm) long on the right side of a pocket section, 4 inches (10 cm) above the lower edge. Mark a similar line on the lining scrap. Place the lining on the right side of the pocket piece, matching the chalked lines. Stitch a rectangle approximately ¼ inch (.7 cm) wide and the length of the marked line, with the chalked line at the center. Cut along the marked line, then clip a V into each corner. Turn the lining to the wrong side and press, having the lining folds even across the opening. On the underside, stitch across the small triangle at each end. On the right side, stitch across in the ditch. Trim the ends of the lining.

The small change pocket is constructed as a separate piece, then folded over the bag edge and stitched in place.

6. Stitch the pocket sections with right sides together. Trim, turn, and press.

7. With wrong sides together, place the lining in the bag.

Position the strap connectors and key tab between the bag and lining against the bag right side. Slip each connector through a ring and fold in half with the ends even. Center them 2 inches (5 cm) from the bag sides, two on the outer bag back and one on the outer bag front, ends aligned with the bag raw edge. Pin the unfinished end of the tab at about the center of the outer bag back.

Keep keys where you can find them quickly. Snap the key ring onto the hook and tuck it into the bag for safekeeping.

8. Pin the lining around the bag opening, the fold just below the bag edge. Topstitch it in place. Stitch across the bag at the halfway point to define the bottom.

9. Fold the change pocket, opening to the bag inside, over the bag upper edge at the position for the remaining strap end. Pin a handle end on top, the end outside the bag. Stitch along the topstitching line.

10. Put the handle ends through the rings, adjust for length, and stitch. Slip the swivel hook onto the key tab, fold the end up and secure it with a button. Sew snaps at the upper corners of the inner bag sections, approximately 2 inches (5 cm) in from the sides and below the upper edge.

Dressed-Up Portfolios

When you walk into a meeting with a portfolio like this one, no one will fail to notice! A business portfolio need not have the same no-nonsense look as your most corporate suit. Design one that works for you—and that will make a lasting impression.

The portfolio holds a standard-size legal pad at the center. On the inner front and back are small pockets, subdivided to hold necessities such as pens, a calculator, and business cards.

Your business portfolio can be as unique as you are. **Design: Grace Grinnell**

Plan the interior pockets to accommodate the items you use most often.

As you can see from the two models, the basic style can be varied in countless ways. Pull out your scrap box and play with combinations until you find one that makes you smile. Add edgings, funky buttons, and extra pockets to make the design all your own.

Open, the portfolio measures 30 inches (76 cm) wide and 14 inches (35.5 cm) high. It folds to 10 by 14 inches (25.5 by 35.5 cm).

SUPPLIES

- Outer fabric: one piece, 30 by 14 inches (76 by 35.5 cm)
- Lining: one piece the size of the outer fabric; two pieces, 11 by 4 inches (28 by 10 cm) for pockets
- Heavy interfacing: two pieces the size of the outer fabric

- Cotton flannel or garment-weight batting: one piece, the size of the outer fabric
- Edge binding: one strip, 90 inches (228 cm) long. Cut it 1½ inches (4 cm) wide if the raw edges can be used, or 2½ inches (6.5 cm) wide if raw edges will be turned under.
- Button or other closure

CONSTRUCTION

1. Fuse or baste one interfacing piece to the wrong side of the outer fabric and one to the lining. Baste the batting to the wrong side of the interfaced outer fabric section.

2. Make a buttonhole on the lining right side for insertion of the cardboard back of a legal pad. Chalk a line 10 inches (25.5 cm) long across the center of the piece, 1½ (4 cm) inches below the upper edge. Work a buttonhole along the line and cut it open.

3.   Make the interior pockets. Hem the upper long edge of each pocket section. Hem the right end of one piece and the left end of the other. Position them at the bottom of each side of the lining, raw edges aligned with the bottom and sides of the lining. Stitch in the seam allowances. Edgestitch the finished ends in place. Add vertical lines of stitching to subdivide the pocket into sections of the desired width.

4.   Sandwich the layers, wrong sides together, and baste around the edges. Press under ½ inch (1.5 cm) on each long edge of the binding, if necessary. Fold the binding over the edges of the portfolio, favoring the lining side slightly. Stitch close to the edge from the outside.

5.   Fold the portfolio in thirds to determine the buttonhole and button positions. Work the buttonhole, and sew on the button.

This variation is made of tussah silk and trimmed with scraps of soft leather. Quilting was worked through all layers, following the lines of the motifs on the lining (below).

Sheer fabric pockets let you find what you need in a hurry.

Computer Case

Statistics say there are more laptops stolen each year than any other item, so why advertise what you are carrying? Made of good linen and embellished with appliqué, this carrier looks more like a designer handbag than the utilitarian case that it is.

The case is designed to hold both computer and adapter. It is lined with foam to protect against bumps. A zippered pocket on the underside of the flap holds diskettes or other small items. The strap is good and wide for wearing comfort.

Inside, the bag measures 16 inches (40.5 cm) wide, 10 inches (25.5 cm) high, and 2¼ inches (5.5 cm) deep.

SUPPLIES

- Fabric: for outer bag, 1 yard (1 m), 45 inches (115 cm) or wider
- For lining: fabric-backed foam, ½ yard (.5 m)
- Pocket fabric: ¼ yard (.25 m)
- Zipper, 7 inches (17.5 cm)
- For appliqué: fabric scraps, paper-backed fusible web

Appliqué decorates the back of the case and the outer flap. Under the flap is a zippered pocket for disks. **Design: Lori Kerr**

CUTTING

1. Cut from fabric two pieces for the outer case front and back, 17½ by 11¾ inches (44 by 30 cm). Cut two side gusset pieces, 4 by 11¾ inches (10 by 30 cm), and one bottom gusset 4 by 17½ inches (10 by 44 cm).

2. Cut two flap sections, 11¾ by 17½ inches (30 by 44 cm). Cut one strap 7¾ by 45 inches (19.5 by 115 cm).

3. From fabric-backed foam, cut two pieces 16¾ by 10⅜ inches (42.5 by 26.5 cm). Cut two pieces 3 by 10⅜ inches (7.5 by 26.5 cm), and one piece 3 by 16¾ inches (7.5 by 42.5 cm).

4. For the pocket, cut one piece 9 by 10 inches (23 by 25 cm), and one piece 9 by 7½ inches (23 by 19 cm).

CONSTRUCTION

Seam allowance is ⅜ inch (1 cm) except as noted.

Appliqué
Plan the appliqué design for the bag back and the upper flap. Apply the fabrics with paper-backed fusible web, following the manufacturer's instructions. Stitch the pieces in place.

Flap
1. Make the pocket for the inner flap. Fold one short edge of the smaller pocket piece to the wrong side and press. Place the pocket sections with right sides together, sides and unfinished ends aligned. Stitch.

2. On the right side of the inner flap piece, chalk a rectangle ½ inch (1.5 cm) high and 7¼ inches (18.5 cm) wide, 2¾ inches (7 cm) below the long edge of the flap and centered between the sides. Stitch on the marked lines with a short stitch length setting. Cut open between the stitching lines, and cut a V at each end to clip close to each corner. Press the cut edges to the wrong side along the stitching lines.

3. Center the zipper, right side up, under the stitched window. Stitch close to the folded edges.

4. Place the pocket behind the zipper, the folded front edge of the pocket along the lower zipper tape. From the flap right side, stitch around the zipper window again ⅜ inch (1 cm) outside the first stitching line, attaching the pocket in the process. Stitch the pocket to the flap across the lower edge.

5. Stitch the flap sections, right sides together, along the sides and outer edge. Begin and end stitching ⅜ inch (1 cm) from the inner flap edge. Trim, and turn. Topstitch the outer edges after the flap is attached to the bag.

Outer Case
1. Stitch a shorter gusset piece to each end of the longer one, right sides together. Press seams open.

2. Join the front and back sections to the gusset strip. Match the seamline intersections at the lower corners to the gusset seamlines. Press the seams open.

3. On the outside, crease and press along each seamline, and topstitch ⅜ inch (1 cm) from the edge through both layers. Do this around the front and back seams, then across the gusset seams. At the top, press the seam extensions toward the gussets. Press under the seam allowance around the opening.

Padded Lining
1. Join the gusset strips as for the outer case.

2. Stitch the front and back to the gusset.

3. Place the lining in the case, wrong sides together, the upper lining ⅜ inch (1 cm) below the pressed upper edge of the case. Fold the pressed edge of the case front and gussets inward over the lining edge, and topstitch in place.

Flap Attachment
1. On the open edge of the flap, press both seam allowances to the wrong side.

2. Undo ⅜ inch (1 cm) at the top of the case back/gusset seam on each side. Slip the flap over the case seam allowance, aligning the seamlines. Edgestitch, then topstitch it in place.

Strap

1. Fold the strap in half lengthwise, wrong sides together, and stitch the long edge and ends, leaving an opening at the center of the long edge. Trim, turn, and press. Topstitch the long edges.

2. Position the strap ends at the inside of each side gusset, the ends approximately 1½ inches (4 cm) below the case edge. Stitch each one in place with a box, then an X.

An attractive carrying case permits your valuable laptop to travel incognito.

Gabardine Portfolio

An elegant portfolio like this one guarantees a good beginning for any important presentation. It's made up in espresso-brown wool gabardine, trimmed with purchased velvet piping and finished with classic gold-tone hardware.

Despite its sleek appearance, it can carry quite a workload. A large pocket on the inner back holds a legal pad or file folders. On its front is a smaller pocket, divided with vertical rows of stitching to organize pens, business cards, and a calculator. The case snaps closed

A wool gabardine business portfolio looks very feminine—and most professional. **Design: Dawn Anderson**

so that another folder or two can be carried between front and back. On the back, a full-length open pocket offers quick access to tickets or the map.

Both the wool and lining are stabilized with lightweight fusible interfacing. Plastic mesh—the kind used for needlework—is incorporated between the layers to provide firm, flexible support. The flip-lock clasp that secures the flap and the strap buckle are available from suppliers of traditional handbag hardware.

SUPPLIES

- Wool gabardine: 1 yard (1 m), 60 inches (152 cm) wide
- Lining fabric: ½ yard (.5 m), 45 inches (115 cm) wide
- Lightweight fusible interfacing: 2½ yards (2.3 m)
- Narrow decorative piping: 6 yards (5.5 m)
- Plastic mesh: three pieces, 10⅝ by 13⅝ inches (27 by 34.5 cm)
- Metal flip-lock bag clasp
- Metal buckle and buckle keeper, ¾ inch (2 cm) width
- Three long eyelets, 3/16 inch (5 mm) diameter, and eyelet tool
- Two large snaps
- Dowel, 3/16-inch (.5-cm) diameter, 13½ inches (34.25 cm) long

CUTTING

1. For portfolio inside and outside, cut from wool two rectangles, 14⅞ by 30¼ inches (37.75 by 76.75 cm). Cut two from interfacing. To create the flap, mark the center of one short end of each rectangle. Mark points on each long side 6 inches (15 cm) from the same short side. Connect the points with a chalk line, and cut along the lines.

2. For the back outer pocket, cut a rectangle 11 by 14⅞ inches (28 by 37.75 cm) from wool and from lining. Cut two from interfacing. For the large interior pocket, cut a rectangle 10½ by 14⅞ inches (26.5 by 37.75 cm) from wool and from lining, and cut two from interfacing. For the small interior pocket, cut a rectangle 5½ by 12⅞ inches (14 by 32.5 cm) from wool and from lining, and two from interfacing.

3. For the strap, cut from wool two strips 1⅜ by 36 inches (4.25 by 91 cm), and two strips 1⅜ by 16½ inches (4.25 by 42 cm). Cut interfacing for all four pieces. Cut a point at one end of each long strip.

CONSTRUCTION

Seam allowance is ½ inch (1.3 cm) except as noted. For best results in pressing wool gabardine, use a damp pressing cloth. A wooden clapper is helpful for smoothing and flattening the seams.

1. Trim seam allowances from the interfacing sections and apply them to the wool and lining pieces according to the manufacturer's instructions.

2. Make the outer pocket. Pin piping to right side of the pocket section along one long edge, aligning the piping stitching line with the fabric. Stitch with a piping or zipper foot. Pin the lining to the pocket with right sides together; stitch just inside previous stitching. Turn right side out and press lightly. Baste the raw edges together.

3. Make the large inner pocket. Right sides together, pin and stitch the wool to the lining along one long edge. Press the seam open. Fold right side out, and press lightly along the seam. Edgestitch. Baste together around the raw edges.

4. Make the small inner pocket. Stitch the pocket and lining, right sides together, along one long edge. Press the seam open, then fold right side out and press to crease along the stitched edge. Refold wrong side out and pin the raw edges together. Stitch, leaving 3 inches (7.5 cm) open along the long edge for turning. Trim seam allowances and corners. Turn right side out. Press, turning under seam allowances along the opening. Edgestitch along the upper edge. Center the pocket on the front of the large inner pocket, the lower edge 1½ inches (4 cm) above the lower edge of the large pocket. Edgestitch it in place. Stitch vertical lines to divide the smaller pocket.

5. Attach the pockets to the inner and outer portfolio sections. On the right side of the inner section, chalk a line parallel to and 11⅞ inches (31.25 cm) from the short

Vertical stitching divides the small interior pocket into compartments sized to suit your needs.

straight edge. Pin the inner pocket to the piece, right sides together, aligning the long raw edge of the pocket with the marked line and with the finished pocket edge toward the flap. Stitch along the marked line. Fold the pocket right side out; press the seam. Baste the pieces together at the sides. Mark the outer portfolio section the same way, and stitch the outer pocket in place. Press and baste as for the inner pocket.

6. Attach piping around the edge of the outer portfolio piece. At the end, remove about ¾ inch (2 cm) of the piping stitching and trim off about ½ inch (1.3 cm) of the cording inside. Fold under the end of the covering ¼ inch (.7 cm) and refold the piping, inserting the remaining end of piping inside the fold to conceal the raw edges. Stitch in place.

7. Pin the inner and outer pieces with right sides together. Stitch just inside previous stitching, leaving the short straight edge open between corners for turning and inserting plastic mesh.

8. Cut a rectangle 6⅜ by 13⅝ inches (16.25 by 34.5 cm) from plastic mesh. Mark the center of one long side. Mark points on the short sides 1 inch (2.5 cm) from the opposite long side. Draw lines to connect the points and cut on the lines. Mark the opening for the clasp, centering it about 1¼ inches (3.5 cm) above the point. Use the opening in the metal clasp as a pattern to cut the hole.

9. Mark the casing for the dowel. On the outside of the portfolio, chalk a line across, 1 inch (2.5 cm) above

A full-length open pocket across the back can accommodate a legal pad or keep tickets handy.

12. Insert the remaining plastic rectangle into the remaining portfolio section. Fold the portfolio and mark the position of the remaining clasp piece on the lower front. Install the clasp, pushing the prongs through just the outer fabric layer and plastic. Press the metal backing over the prongs and fold prongs over to secure. Slipstitch the opening.

13. Mark the snap positions on the inside of the portfolio, approximately ¾ inch (2 cm) below the dowel casing and 1 inch (2.5 cm) in from the sides. Cover the snap sections with lining fabric and stitch them in place. Cover the remaining sections and sew them in the corresponding positions on the lower flap.

14. Make the straps. Pin piping around the outer edges of one longer strap piece, beginning and ending ½ inch (1.5 cm) from the straight end. At the ends, remove the piping stitching for about ¾ inch (2 cm); trim away about ½ inch (1.3 cm) of the cord, and fold ¼ inch (.5 cm) of the piping to the wrong side. Stitch the piping. Trim seam allowances to a scant ⅜ inch (1 cm). Apply piping to the long edges of one shorter strap piece in the same way, finishing the ends as described above.

15. Stitch around the remaining strap pieces a scant ½ inch (1.2 cm) from the raw edges. Fold on the stitched lines and press to the wrong side. Trim seam allowances to ¼ inch (.5 cm). Pin these pieces to the piped pieces. Slipstitch in place.

16. Attach the buckle and eyelets. On the short strap section, make a ⅜-inch (1-cm) buttonhole 1½ inches (4 cm) from one end. Insert the buckle prong through the buttonhole and fold the strap around it. Stitch the strap layers together, stitching close to the buckle. Insert the keeper between the strap layers about ½ inch (1.5 cm) from the buckle end. Stitch close to edge of keeper. Install the eyelets in the longer strap, beginning about 3½ inches (9 cm) from the pointed end and placing the others 1⅛ inches (3 cm) apart. Hand stitch the other end of each strap to the dowel casing on the inside of the portfolio.

the pocket opening. Draw a second line a scant ¾ (2 cm) above the first. Insert the plastic mesh piece into the flap end against the outer fabric. Stitch along the casing line closest to the plastic.

10. Chalk mark the opening for the clasp on the flap front. Work machine or hand satin stitch around the marked opening, and trim away fabric inside the stitching. Install the clasp.

11. Insert the dowel into the casing area. Pin the portfolio sections together along casing line. Stitch on second casing line, enclosing the dowel. Insert a plastic mesh rectangle, 10⅝ by 13⅝ inches (27 by 34.5 cm), between the portfolio layers. Pin layers together along the ditch formed by the pocket seamlines; stitch through all layers.

Travel Plans

Whether your travel plans involve a day's shopping expedition, a fast business trip, or a glorious month-long vacation at an exotic destination, it is easier to focus on the real purpose of the journey when your gear is securely packed and well organized at the start. Here are plenty of suggestions for keeping your travel essentials in order in the prettiest possible way. From cash carriers to spacious duffels, you'll find solutions to all the packing problems. There are lots of gift ideas for traveling friends, too!

Postcard Packet

W hat could be a more thoughtful gift for a friend about to leave on vacation? A pretty postcard kit, complete with address labels, stamps, cards, and a pen, takes up little luggage space and leaves vacation time free for touring.

Sewing room scraps will provide all the necessary fabric, and the creative potential is nearly limitless. We've shown two variations, one pieced from scraps far too small to use for anything else. And it's a good opportunity to experiment with decorative stitches and

threads—it's almost impossible to go wrong. The finished case, closed, is 6½ inches (16.5 cm) wide and 4¾ inches (12 cm) high.

SUPPLIES

- Fabric: two pieces, 7 by 10 inches (17.5 by 25 cm), for outer cover and lining. One pocket piece 7 by 4¼ inches (17.5 by 11 cm), and one piece 7 by 3½ inches (17.5 by 9 cm)

A colorful patchwork portfolio makes it fun to get those postcards written. The cover was pieced using the flip technique, described in step 1 on page 78. **Design: Daphne Piester**

Small interior pockets hold stamps and business cards. Hems are sewn with machine embroidery stitches and decorative threads.

- Fusible interfacing: two pieces, 7 by 10 inches (17.5 by 25 cm)
- Elastic piece: narrow to medium width, 1¼ inches (3 cm) long
- Small hook and loop tape button or other closure

CONSTRUCTION

Seam allowance is ¼ inch (.5 cm). Note: if you piece fabrics for the cover, make the patchwork slightly larger than you will need, then trim it to the cover size.

1. Apply interfacing to the wrong side of the cover and lining pieces.

2. Stitch a ¼-inch (.5-cm) double hem along one long edge of each pocket piece. Use a decorative stitch and ornamental thread if you wish. Place the smaller pocket, right side up, on the right side of the larger pocket with lower raw edges and sides even; pin. Approximately 3 inches (7.5 cm) from the right edge, stitch a vertical line to divide the smaller pocket into sections.

3. Place the pockets, right side up, on the lining right side, lower edges even. Baste in the seam allowance.

4. Stitch the ends of the elastic together to form a loop that will hold a pen snugly. Fold the lining in half across to mark the center, and sew the loop in place there.

5. With right sides together, stitch the lining to the outer cover, leaving an opening at one side for turning. Trim, turn, and press. Stitch the opening. Apply a snap or other closure to the flap lining and at the lower front.

Pretty luggage adds an element of fun to any trip. **Design: Tracy Munn**

Travel Trio

Duffels in two sizes with a hanging bag to match will take you away in grand style. With these colorful fabrics, there is no chance of another traveler picking up your bag by mistake. We have used sturdy cotton, backed with firm fusible interfacing. With complementary patterns like these, the main fabric for one piece can be used as trim on the other, and vice versa. Decorator cottons would work well for this set. Many are treated with a stain-resistant finish, a plus for travel gear. Tapestry fabric and heavy linen are other fabrics to consider.

The duffel bags zip across the tops, and have pockets at both ends. The front and back pockets are actually a single piece, attached at the sides by the straps and stitched in place across the bottom.

The garment bag has a zipper down one side. There is a shoulder strap across the center so that the bag can be folded double for carrying. A ribbon tie at the top keeps the hangers together, and two more ribbons can be tied through loops on the bottom of the bag when the bag is folded.

Large Duffel
The finished bag is 21 inches (53 cm) wide, 17 inches (43 cm) high, and 9 inches (23 cm) deep at the base.

SUPPLIES

- Fabric: 2¼ yards (2.1 m), 54 inches (137 cm) wide. Allow additional for contrast pocket trim.
- Firm fusible interfacing: 3 yards (2.75 m)
- Strap webbing: 3 yards (2.75 m), 1¼ inches (3 cm) wide
- Piping cord: 2¼ yards (2.1 m), ¼ inch (.7 cm) diameter
- Zipper, 20 inches (50.5 cm)

CUTTING

1. Enlarge the pattern for the bag end (page 102) and cut it from paper.

2. Cut one main bag piece, 41 by 22 inches (104 by 56 cm). Cut interfacing this size.

3. With the pattern, cut two ends from bag fabric and two from interfacing.

4. Cut one central pocket, 35 by 12 inches (89 by 30 cm). Cut interfacing this size.

5. Cut two end pockets, 17 by 10½ inches (43 by 26.5 cm). To shape the pocket, fold the fabric in half crosswise. Place the pattern on the doubled fabric, lining up the raw edges opposite the fabric fold with the pattern lower edge. Trim the sides and lower corners to the pattern.

6. Cut bias strips for piping 1½ inches (4 cm) wide. Piece strips as necessary to obtain two lengths, each 1⅛ yards (1.05 m).

CONSTRUCTION

Use ½ inch (1.5 cm) seam allowances.

1. Following the manufacturer's instructions, apply interfacing to the wrong sides of the bag main section, ends, and central pocket. To mark the bottom of the bag, bring the two short ends of the central piece together and press the resulting fold.

2. Make the central pocket. Clean finish the two short ends. Fold each 3 inches (8 cm) to the wrong side; stitch the hems. Apply a strip of contrast trim across each hemmed edge, if desired. Bring the hemmed edges together and press a crease across the bottom to mark the center of the piece.

3. Center the pocket on the central piece, matching bottom creases. Zigzag in place along the sides. Stitch along the bottom crease, then stitch again approximately 2 inches (5 cm) to each side of the first stitching line.

4. Attach the handles. Beginning at the bottom crease on the main section, pin the webbing to cover the pocket edge. Pin to a point 1 inch (2.5 cm) above the upper edge of the pocket, then leave a loop 22 inches

Try a mix of complementary fabrics for bags that look great alone or together.

(56 cm) long for the handle, and resume pinning 1 inch (2.5 cm) above the other side of the pocket. Pin webbing to cover that pocket edge all the way around the bottom of the bag to the upper edge on the other side, then make the other handle and continue to the starting point. Fold under the end. Stitch in place along both edges of the webbing.

5. Install the zipper. Center the zipper along one short end of the main piece with right sides together. Stitch along the zipper tape stitching line. Stitch the other end of the piece to the other zipper tape. On one side, fold a pleat parallel to the zipper and ⅝ inch (1.5 cm) from the fabric edge to create an overlap. Stitch the pleat in place along the zipper tape. On the other side, press the seam flat. Close the zipper, and baste across the ends.

6. Baste a pocket to each end section.

7. Make the piping. Cut the cording in half. Fold a bias strip right side out around a length of piping cord and stitch close to the cord. Pin to the right side of one end section, raw edges together and seamlines matched. Clip the piping seam allowance around curves as necessary. Overlap the ends by about 1 inch (2.5 cm). Stitch in place, leaving about 2 inches (5 cm) unstitched at the ends. Remove the stitching at one end of the piping and trim the cord so the cord ends meet. Fold under ½ inch (1.3 cm) of fabric and fold it around the remaining end of the piping. Finish the stitching.

8. With right sides together, pin the end sections to the bag. Stitch just inside the piping stitching line. Clean finish the seam allowances.

Small Duffel

The finished bag is 14 inches (35.5 cm) wide, 10 inches (25.5 cm) high, and 8 inches (20 cm) deep at the base. It has a shoulder strap in addition to the handles.

SUPPLIES

- Fabric: 1½ yards (1.4 m), 54 inches (137 cm) wide. Allow additional for contrast pocket trim.
- Firm fusible interfacing: 2¼ yards (2.1 m)
- Strap webbing: 3⅞ yards (3.55 m), 1¼ inches (3 cm) wide
- Piping cord: 1⅞ yards (1.75 m), ¼ inch (.7 cm) diameter
- Zipper, 12 inches (30.5 cm)

CUTTING

1. Enlarge the pattern for the bag end (page 102) and cut it from paper.

2. Cut one main bag piece, 33 by 15 inches (84 by 38 cm). Cut interfacing this size.

3. With the pattern, cut two ends from bag fabric and two from interfacing.

4. Cut one central pocket, 25 by 8½ inches (63 by 21.5 cm). Cut interfacing this size.

5. Cut two end pockets, 13 by 9¼ inches (33 by 23.5 cm). To shape the pocket, fold the fabric in half crosswise. Place the pattern on the doubled fabric, lining up the raw edges opposite the fabric fold with the pattern lower edge. Trim the sides and lower corners to the pattern.

6. Cut bias strips for piping 1½ inches (4 cm) wide. Piece strips as necessary to obtain two lengths, each 33 inches (84 cm).

CONSTRUCTION

Make the bag according to the instructions for the large duffel through step 3. Cut webbing 75 inches (190 cm) long. Attach the webbing as described in step 4, but leave 20 inches (51 cm) of webbing unstitched for each handle.

Attach the shoulder strap after the bag is finished. Fold the remaining length of webbing in half. Stitch an end of the doubled strip toward the top of each end of the bag, stitching a 1-inch (2.5-cm) X to secure it.

Garment Bag

The finished bag is 23 inches (58.5 cm) wide, 43 inches (109 cm) long, and 2½ inches (6.5 cm) deep.

SUPPLIES

- Bag fabric: 1½ yards (1.4 m), 54 or 60 inches (137 or 152 cm) wide
- Contrast fabric for piping: 7½ yards (6.9 m) of bias strips 1½ inches (4 cm) wide
- Small scrap of contrast fabric for loops
- Piping cord: 7½ yards (6.9 m), ¼ inch (.7 cm) diameter
- Grosgrain ribbon: 3 yards (2.75 m), 1 inch (2.5 cm) wide
- Strap webbing: 48 inches (122 cm), 1¼ inches (3.5 cm) wide
- Zipper: 38 inches (96 cm). Upholstery supply shops can cut zippers to specified lengths.

The garment bag folds in half and ties with ribbons through loops at the lower edge.

CUTTING

1. For the bag front and back, cut two pieces 43 by 24 inches (109 by 61 cm). Use a hanger as a template to shape the slope of the shoulders at the top of each piece. Use a mug or other object to slightly round the upper and lower corners. Mark top center of each piece.

2. Cut a side gusset strip 81 by 3½ inches (206 by 9 cm), or piece strips to this length. For the zipper gusset, cut two pieces 2¼ by 39½ inches (5.5 by 100.5 cm).

3. Cut two strips for loops, 4½ inches (11.5 cm) long and 2 inches (5 cm) wide.

CONSTRUCTION

Seam allowances are ½ inch (1.5 cm).

1. Make loops for tying the bag closed. Fold each strip in half lengthwise, right side out, and press. Fold the raw edges in to center and press again. Edgestitch both long edges. Fold each piece in half and position on the lower edge of the bag back right side, 5 inches (12.5 cm) from each corner, ends even with the bag edge and approximately ¾ inch (2 cm) apart. Baste.

2. Cut the ribbon into three equal lengths. Fold two of these in half, and pin the folded edge to the upper edge of the bag back right side, 5 inches (12.5 cm) from each corner, the folded edges even with the bag edge.

3. Double the webbing and position it across the bag back at the halfway point. Stitch the ends securely in place at the sides.

4. Baste the zipper gusset strips right sides together along one long edge. Press open. Place the zipper face down over the seam wrong side and stitch twice along each side. Stitch across the seam below the lower end of the zipper. Remove the basting. Stitch the lower end of the zipper gusset to the remaining gusset strip, right sides together. Press the seam allowances downward and topstitch them in place.

5. To bind the gusset ends, cut two strips of main or contrast fabric 2½ inches (6.5 cm) long and 2 inches (5 cm) wide. Cut one strip 3½ inches (9 cm) long and the same width. Fold under the seam allowance at one end of each of the shorter strips; press. Fold and press all the strips as for the loops in step 1. Bind the upper ends of the zipper gusset with the two shorter strips. Put the other aside.

6. Make piping. Cut the cording in half. Fold a bias strip right side out around a length of cord and stitch close to the cord. Beginning at the bottom, pin to the right side of one bag section, raw edges together and seamlines matched. Clip the piping seam allowance around curves as necessary. Overlap the ends by approximately 1 inch (2.5 cm). Stitch in place, leaving about 2 inches (5 cm) unstitched at the ends. Remove the stitching at one end of the piping and trim the cord so the cord ends meet. Fold under ½ inch (1.3 cm) of fabric and fold it around the remaining end of the piping. Finish the stitching. Stitch to the other bag section in the same way.

7. Beginning at top center and with the zipper end of the gusset, pin the gusset to one bag section with right sides together, keeping the ribbon ends free. Stitch to within approximately 3 inches (7.5 cm) of the end. Match the gusset seam to the bag, and trim the gusset end if necessary. Bind the end, then finish the seam. Pin and stitch the other bag section in place.

8. Fold the remaining length of ribbon in half. Stitch the folded end to the underside of the gusset edge binding opposite the zipper.

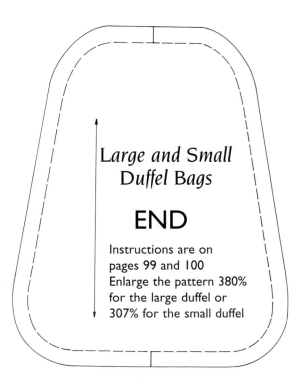

Large and Small Duffel Bags

END

Instructions are on pages 99 and 100 Enlarge the pattern 380% for the large duffel or 307% for the small duffel

Security Pocket

Our grandmothers often used these, and they are once again a good idea. The tiny fabric envelope tucks in the bra front to keep cash safe and attaches to the bra straps with narrow ribbons. It is a quick gift to make for a friend about to embark on a journey.

Make the pocket as pretty as lingerie with a scrap of cotton batiste, silk, or any soft fabric. Add decorative stitching and a monogram as we have done, or perhaps a miniature appliqué. Remember to choose soft ribbon, too.

SUPPLIES

- Fabric: two pieces, 4¾ inches (12 cm) wide and 9½ inches (24 cm) long
- Narrow ribbon: 19 inches (48 cm)
- Hook and loop tape: a small piece, or
- Three very small clear snaps

A special cash pocket fits into the traditional hiding place for a woman's money.
Design: Daphne Piester

CONSTRUCTION

1. Mark the center of both pieces at one end. Mark a point 2½ inches from that end on each side. Connect the marks to make the point at the end of the pieces.

2. Stitch the pieces with right sides together and ¼ inch (.5 cm) seam allowance, leaving an opening at the bottom for turning. Trim, turn, and press.

3. Fold the lower third of the piece upward to the base of the point. Center the ribbon across the front of the piece approximately 1 inch (2.5 cm) below the edge of the opening. Stitch the sides, stitching the ribbon in place at the same time. Use a decorative stitch and contrasting thread if desired. Add a monogram to the flap if you wish.

4. With the pocket in place, check the spacing between the bra straps.

Fold a ribbon end around each strap and trim the ends, if necessary, for a loop of approximately 1½ inches (4 cm). Turn under each end of the ribbon ⅜ inch (1 cm). Stitch a snap section or very small piece of hook and loop tape to cover the ribbon end. Stitch the corresponding snap or tape section along the ribbon.

5. Sew another snap under the flap point.

Cassette Folder

M usic makes car travel far more pleasant, but keeping track of tapes and their cases can dampen the pleasure. A cleverly designed fabric holder provides a snug compartment for each tape and folds up accordion style. An elasticized outer loop slips around the folded carrier to keep it together.

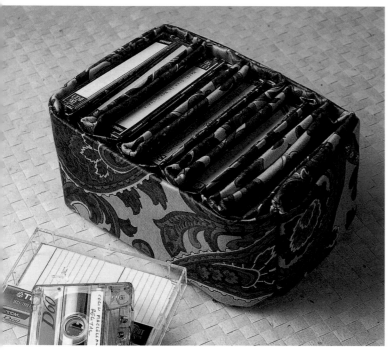

An accordion-pleated fabric envelope keeps cassettes orderly, their titles visible for quick selection. **Design: Lori Kerr**

Cotton fabric, left over from a decorating project, is just right for this folder. It's pretty—and it has a soil-resistant finish that is always an advantage with travel gear. The folder holds nine standard cassettes in their cases.

SUPPLIES

- Cotton fabric: one piece 52 inches (132 cm) long and 14 inches (35.5 cm) wide, and one piece 24 inches (61 cm) long by 7 inches (18 cm) wide
- Elastic: 23 inches (58.5 cm) long, 2 to 2½ inches (5 to 6.5 cm) wide

CONSTRUCTION

Use ½ inch (1.5 cm) seam allowance.

1. Fold the longer fabric in half lengthwise, right sides together, and stitch. Press the seam open; turn right side out. Press under the seam allowances at both ends. Fold the piece in half lengthwise again, with the seam inside. Stitch one end closed, stitching close to the edge then ¼ inch (.5 cm) in.

2. Fold the second fabric piece in half lengthwise, right sides together, and stitch. Press, and turn right side out. Slip the elastic through the piece and stitch securely at each end in the seam allowance. Fold the piece in half, short ends together and the seam inside, and baste.

3. Fold the open ends of the longer piece over the raw ends of the shorter piece, aligning the seamlines. Stitch with two rows of stitching.

4. Divide the longer piece into sections. Chalk mark perpendicular lines across it at 5⅜-inch (14.25-cm) intervals. Use a cassette box to check. Stitch along the marked line

An elasticized outer loop slips off for easy access to the tapes.

Disc Carrier

Designed to hold a handful of CDs or cassettes, this compact case is a great traveling companion for short trips. It is quick to make up in any pretty fabric, and gets top ratings as a gift.

The two versions shown are made of medium-weight cotton, one self-lined and one lined with a harmonizing print. A remnant of interesting trim or braid makes a perfect handle. For the front closure, use a hook and loop tape button, add a one-of-a-kind button and a buttonhole in the flap, or dream up a unique closure of your own.

It can accommodate either CDs or cassettes, and it can be made up quickly with a small amount of fabric. It is a perfect gift!
Design: Judith Robertson

SUPPLIES

- Fabric: approximately ¼ yard (.25 m) of outer fabric and of lining
- Fusible interfacing to suit fabric: 20 by 3⅜ inches (51 by 9 cm)
- Trim or cord for handle: 11 inches (28 cm) long
- Elastic: ¼ inch (.7 cm) wide, 8½ inches (21.5 cm) long
- Button, hook and loop tape, or other closure

CUTTING

1. For the central section, cut one outer piece and one lining, 20 by 3⅜ inches (51 by 9 cm). Trim the corners diagonally from the flap end of each piece.

2. Cut two side pieces from outer fabric and two from lining, 6 by 3⅜ inches (15 by 9 cm).

CONSTRUCTION

Seam allowance is ⅜ inch (1 cm) except as noted.

1. Following manufacturer's instructions, apply interfacing to the wrong side of the outer bag central section.

2. With the short ends of both pieces even, sew a side piece (6-inch or 15-cm side) to one side of the central piece, right sides together, stopping at the seamline at the other short end. Pivot, and sew the short end of the side piece along the side of the central piece as shown, again stopping at the seamline. Pivot again, and sew the third edge of the side piece to the central piece, this time sewing to the edge. Sew the other

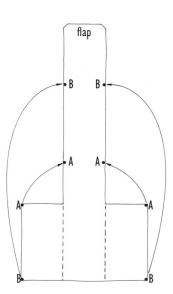

side piece in the same way to the other long edge of the central section. Repeat with the lining pieces.

3. With right sides together, stitch the flap to the flap lining. Trim, turn, and press. Topstitch around the flap edges. Tuck the lining into the bag, wrong sides together.

4. To make a channel for the elastic, stitch the bag and lining together around the opening 1⅛ inches (3 cm) below the upper edge. Press bag and lining edges ½ inch (1.3 cm) to the wrong side, having the upper folded edges even. Place the elastic in the channel. Secure it to the back seam allowance at one end.

5. Pin the ends of the handle in place between the bag and lining at each side of the bag. Stitch the bag and lining together close to the upper edges, pulling the elastic gently along as you go. Secure the elastic at the other end and finish closing the channel.

6. Work a buttonhole in the flap and sew a button onto the bag front, or add the closure of your choice.

Hobbies & Games

Biking or bridge, sewing or sketching—it seems every pastime calls for at least a few materials or tools that must occasionally be carried from place to place. We sewers are lucky! Instead of cruising the malls or paging through mail-order catalogs to find a carryall that works, we can create one that's made to order.

The models in this chapter represent a range of special activities and ways to accommodate the gear they require. If your own interests are not included here, look at the photos and instructions for ideas on how you might design your own custom carrier. The designers have devised some very clever techniques for dealing with special needs.

The sewer's tote unzips at one end for easy access to the contents. **Design: Mary Parker**

The Sewer's Tote

For attending classes or packing up to spend the afternoon sewing with a friend, a specially designed tote keeps all the sewing tools and accessories together, organized so you can find the one you need at the moment. There is plenty of room for the current project and pattern, too.

As a bonus, the bag unzips down one end to reveal the contents. Foamcore stiffens the sides and bottom to make the bag sturdy. Interior pockets span the sides and closed end of the bag. You can arrange and subdivide them to accommodate your own tools.

The finished tote is 14 inches (35.5 cm) wide, 7 inches (18 cm) deep, and 13 inches (33 cm) high.

SUPPLIES

- Fabric: sturdy cotton or cotton blend in the following colors: Green, ½ yard (.5 m); black, 1 yard (.95 m); red, ⅝ yard (.6 m), and blue, ¼ yard (.25 m)
- Separating sports zipper, 12 to 14 inches (30.5 to 35.3 cm)long (see step 12)
- Hook and loop tape: 6 inches (15 cm)
- Foamcore: 1 piece, 24 by 36 inches (61 by 91.5 cm)
- Webbing, 1 inch (2.5 cm) wide: 2 yards (1.85 m)

CUTTING

1. From green fabric, cut the tote upper section, 42½ by 9¼ inches (108 by 23.5 cm). Cut the lining bottom, 15½ by 8 inches (39.5 by 20 cm).

2. From black fabric, cut the tote lower section/lining, 42½ by 19 inches (108 by 48 cm). Cut the outer bottom piece, 15½ by 8 inches (39.5 by 20 cm).

3. From red fabric, cut two pocket pieces 11½ by 14 inches (29 by 35.5 cm). Cut two pieces 6½ by 14 inches (16.5 by 35.5 cm).

4. From blue fabric, cut one pocket piece 8½ by 7 inches (21.5 by 17.5 cm).

5. Cut two pieces of foamcore for the bag front and back, 13¾ by 12½ inches (35 by 31.5 cm). Cut one piece for the non-zipper end, 6⅜ by 13¾ inches (16 by 34.5 cm). Cut one piece for the bottom, 6¼ by 13¾ inches (15.5 by 34.5 cm).

CONSTRUCTION

Seam allowance is ⅜ inch (1 cm) except as noted.

1. Lay out the tote upper section right side up. Along the lower edge, measure from the left end and mark at 6½ and 15½ inches (16.5 and 39.5 cm). Measure and mark the same intervals from the right end. Position the handles. Position the ends of one webbing strip over the first marks, ends even with the fabric edge. Place the second strip over the remaining marks. Pin the lower 8 inches (20 cm) of each strap in place. Stitch the ends securely in the seam allowance, and stitch along the edges of each pinned section.

2. Pin the lower tote/lining piece to the upper section along the edge with the handle ends, right sides together. Stitch, and press the seam open. Fold the piece in half lengthwise, right side out, and press the fold. The crease will indicate the lower edge of the tote.

3. Prepare the pockets. Fold and stitch a narrow double hem along one long edge of each red pocket section, and on one short edge of the blue pocket. With both pieces right side up, position each smaller red pocket on a larger one, lower edges even. Baste together ½ inch (1.5 cm) from the edges. Press the raw edges of all pieces ½ inch (1.5 cm) to the wrong side.

4. Lay out the tote piece, right side up and the black fabric (the lining) upward. Mark the center of the upper edge and extend the line downward approximately 13 inches (33 cm).

5. Position the blue pocket. Fold it in half lengthwise and align the fold with the marked line. Unfold the pocket and pin it in place, the upper edge 1½ inches (4 cm) below the tote upper edge. Pin a red pocket to each side of the blue one, ¾ inch (2 cm) away, the upper edges even. Topstitch the pockets in place. On the red pockets, stitch vertical lines to divide into sections.

6. Fold the piece in half, right sides together, along the center crease. Stitch the long edges. Press the seam open and turn right side out. On the lining side, mark the midpoint of the piece at the seam and on the raw edge.

7. Stitch the bottom pieces, right sides together, along the long sides and one short end, using ¼ inch (.5 cm) seam allowance. Trim, turn, and press.

8. Pin the bottom section to the tote sides. Pin with right sides together, beginning at the center of the sewn short end of the bottom, matching it to the marked point on the tote. Leave the unsewn end of the bottom and the open end of the tote free. Stitch around the three sides with ½ inch (1.3 cm) seam allowance. Press the seam allowance toward the tote sides.

9. Fit the foamcore end piece between the outer tote and lining at the closed end, trimming if necessary. Position it directly behind the blue pocket. Using a zipper foot, stitch as closely as possible along both sides of the foamcore to enclose it. Insert the other two pieces of foamcore in the sides, forcing them close to the stitching at the back corners. Stitch each piece in place as for the first piece.

10. At the open end, turn the side and lower raw edges ⅜ inch (1 cm) to the wrong side and press. Stitch across each lower edge.

11. Insert the remaining piece of foamcore in the bottom. Turn the seam allowances to the inside and edgestitch along the folded edges to close the end.

12. Stitch the zipper in place. At the upper end, miter the corner of the tape and stitch along the upper edge on each side as shown on the model. As an alternative, cut off the excess and stitch a small scrap of seam binding over the uppermost teeth on each side to stop the zipper pull.

13. Cut one hook and loop tape section in half and sew a piece along the lower lining edge at each side of the zipper opening. Sew the other section along the open edge of the tote bottom.

Plenty of pockets keep tools and notions well organized.

Bike Bag

Designed for the short rides around town, this compact bag holds keys, a nutrition bar, and a few other small essentials. It attaches snugly under the seat with a buttoned loop. The opening is placed at an end so the contents are accessible while the bag is in place.

The bag is 6 inches (15 cm) long and 3½ inches (9 cm) in diameter. This model is made of heavy denim, trimmed and stitched in red for contrast.

SUPPLIES

- Fabric: ¼ yard (.25 m)
- Fusible interfacing: ¼ yard (.25 m)
- Three buttons

CUTTING

1. Enlarge the pattern pieces on page 118 and cut them from paper.

2. From the patterns, cut one piece each from fabric and interfacing.

3. For the main bag section, cut one rectangle, 7 by 15 inches (17.5 by 38 cm), from fabric and one from interfacing.

4. For the button strap, cut one piece, 3 by 9 inches (7.5 by 23 cm).

CONSTRUCTION

Seam allowance is ½ inch (1.3 cm) except as noted.

1. Fuse interfacing to the wrong sides of the fabric pieces.

2. Mark buttonhole placement in the center of the main bag piece to align with the metal loops under the bike seat.

3. Make the button strap. Fold the strip in half, lengthwise, wrong side out. Stitch the ends and long

The small bag fastens securely under the seat to carry essentials during short rides. **Design: Kate Mathews**

edge, leaving an opening for turning. Trim, turn, and press. Close the opening. Work a buttonhole at each end to fit the buttons.

4. Work buttonholes at the marked points on the main bag piece, their length to accommodate the strap.

5. With right sides together, join the short ends of the bag to form a tube. Press the seam open.

6. With right sides together, stitch the full circle into one end of the bag. It may be helpful to baste first, then stitch slowly, pivoting as necessary with the needle in the fabric. Grade the seam allowances.

7. Turn under and stitch the seam allowances on the straight edges of both partial circles. Overlap the pieces to form a circle and baste in the seam allowances. Stitch the piece into the open end of the bag. Turn right side out.

8. Attach a button loop and button to the open end. Thread the strap ends through the metal loops on the bike seat and button in place.

Spa Bag

In spite of its name, this bag is far too practical to have such a singular purpose. Vinyl is fused to the outer fabric to make it waterproof and more durable. It's a great size to use for the beach, for a weekend trip, or for about anything else that calls for a roomy carryall.

Two zippers in the side gusset meet at the top so the bag can be opened part way without spilling its contents. Webbing handles are long enough that the bag can be carried over your shoulder. A lining of thin, dense foam helps protect breakables inside the bag.

Fusible vinyl? It works! Vinyl was applied to the outer fabric used for this bag. For a moisture-proof interior, it could as easily be applied to the lining fabric. **Design: Lori Kerr**

With the fabric scraps, you might make one or two companion bags to contain small items. One easy version is the window case described on page 126. You might also add pockets to the foam lining pieces before stitching them in place. See the suggestions in the Introduction.

The bag measures 13 inches (33 cm) wide, 14 inches (35.5 cm) high, and 5½ inches (14 cm) deep.

SUPPLIES

- Fabric for outer bag: 1 yard (1 m) medium-weight cotton
- Contrast fabric for trim: 2 strips, 7 by 42 inches (17.5 by 106.5 cm)
- Fusible vinyl: 2 yards (1.85 m)
- Fabric-backed foam: 2 pieces, 15½ by 13½ inches (39.5 by 34 cm)
- Webbing, 1 inch (2.5 cm) wide: 1½ yards (1.4 m)
- Two 20-inch (50.5-cm) zippers

CUTTING

1. For the bag front and back, cut two pieces of outer fabric and two of vinyl, 16½ by 14½ inches (42 by 36.5 cm). On the fabric, mark the center of each short edge to indicate center top and bottom.

2. For the side gussets, cut two strips of outer fabric and two of vinyl, 7 by 42 inches (17.5 by 106.5 cm).

CONSTRUCTION

Seam allowances are ⅜ inch (1 cm) except as noted.

1. Following manufacturer's instructions, fuse vinyl to the right sides of the outer fabric pieces.

2. Stitch the gusset sections together at one end with right sides together. Press the seam allowances to one side and topstitch them in place. Stitch the contrast trim pieces in the same way.

3. The zippers will be installed in a window in the gusset, with the contrast trim providing a narrow "frame." First, fold the outer fabric strip in half lengthwise and press a crease to mark the center. On the wrong side, chalk a line ¼ inch (.5 cm) to either side of the crease. Extend the lines 20 inches (50.5 cm) in each direction from the seam. Connect the lines with a horizontal line at each end. Place the strip and the contrast strip with right sides together. Stitch around the window. Cut an opening between the stitching lines, cutting along the pressed crease, then in a V shape into the corners. Turn and press, allowing the contrast fabric to extend slightly to the right side around the window.

4. Trim away the excess tape at the upper end of each zipper. Join them, head to head, by stitching the tapes together at the top.

5. Position the zippers with the join at the seamline of the gusset strip (top center of the bag). Center them under the window, and stitch just outside the visible trim. Stitch again approximately ¼ inch (.5 cm) away.

6. Beginning at top center, stitch the zipper strip to one bag section. Stitch each side to a point on the lower edge about 2 inches (5 cm) past each corner. Carefully match the length of the gusset strip to the bag seamline, then trim off the excess at each end of the gusset, stitch the ends together, and topstitch the seam allowances in place. Finish stitching the gusset to the bag. Stitch the other bag piece in place. Press the seam allowances toward the gusset.

7. Add pockets to the foam lining sections, if you wish. Place a lining section in the bag against one side, under the seam allowances. Trim the foam, if necessary, so it does not extend beyond the seamline at any point. On the outside, Fold along the outer seamline and stitch through all layers ⅜ inch (1 cm) from the first seam. This holds the foam in place and creates a border around the outer edge of the bag. Stitch the other side in the same manner.

8. Attach the straps. Cut the webbing in half and clean finish the ends. On the outside of the bag, attach an end at each side gusset, stitching approximately 2 inches (5 cm) of the strap at the upper end of the gusset. Stitch an X to reinforce each one.

Artists' Paraphernalia Pockets

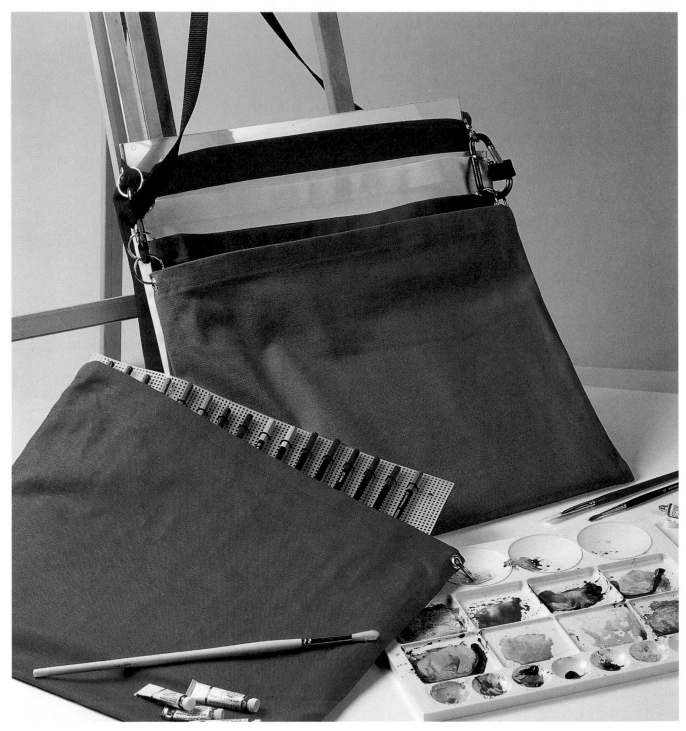

On this artist's portfolio, pockets can be added when they're needed and removed when they're not. When the materials exceed the portfolio's capacity, a new pocket can be stitched up in less than an hour. **Design: Dee Dee Triplett**

Colorful giant-sized pockets hold all the artist's gear, each material in a pocket of its own. Take only those you will need for today's class or outing, clasp them onto the strap, and you're ready to go. They provide a great way to keep your supplies in order at home, too.

The pockets are open across the top. We have added a custom mesh rack for paint tubes to one of the pockets, with an elastic cord that weaves in and out of the mesh to keep the tubes secure.

Each pocket is 14 by 18 inches (35.5 by 46 cm).

SUPPLIES

- Webbing, 1¼ inches (3.5 cm) wide: 1½ yards (1.4 m)
- Two 32 mm split rings (key rings)
- Two carabiners, 3 inches (7.5 cm) long
For each pocket you will need:
- Heavy poplin or similar fabric, 24 by 36 inches (61 by 91.5 cm)
- Two eyelets, ½ inch (1.3 cm) diameter

CONSTRUCTION

1. Cut fabric to 20 by 32 inches (51 by 81.5 cm). Fold in half, right side out, to 16 by 20 inches (40.5 by 51 cm). Stitch the short ends with French seams: sew with ¼ inch (.7 cm) seam allowance (wrong sides are together). Trim the seam allowances and press open. With right sides together, fold and press along the seamline. Stitch with ½ inch (1.3 cm) seam allowance. Cut away the thick seam allowances only under the hem to prevent breaking a machine needle when you stitch the hem.

2. Stitch a 1-inch (2.5-cm) double hem around the top opening. Install the eyelets at each side of the top, through both layers of the hem. Place a split ring through each eyelet.

3. For the carrying strap, determine a comfortable length. Sew a loop at each end of the webbing.

4. To carry the pockets, place the rings on the carabiners, loop a carabiner through each strap loop, and you're equipped to go.

Paintbrush Pocket Variation

Instead of a top opening, this pocket has a flap and inner pockets to hold brushes—or pens, markers and similar tools. A long strip of hook and loop tape secures the flap.

1. Cut the main piece as for the plain pockets, but press hems at the sides rather than stitching the edges together. Cut pockets slightly narrower than the width of the main pocket, and not as high. For more interesting results, cut the pocket upper edge on the diagonal as this designer has done, and use an assortment of colors.

2. Hem the upper edge of each pocket. Stitch the sections together, beginning by stitching the front (shortest) pocket to the one behind it, and so on. Use the stitching lines to subdivide the pocket as well as to hold the layers together.

3. Stitch the hook and loop tape at the lower edge, allowing for the hem width of the main piece.

4. Lay out the joined pockets on the inside of the main piece. Trim the pocket edges, if necessary, so the piece fits under the pressed hem. Stitch the hem, catching the sides and lower edges of the pocket section.

Change the pocket design slightly to make a special carrier for paintbrushes and the like.

Playing Card Carrier

Those who love to play bridge appreciate the gift of a traveling card case. This one has plenty of pockets and holders for everything a great game requires: a double deck, scorepad, individual tallies, and a pencil or two. Make one for yourself at the same time. It's a handy way to keep everything together so you are ready for a game at short notice.

Because cards and pads vary in size, we have given specific instructions and measurements for just the outer case. The inner pockets can then be tailored to fit your needs. The outer case, closed, is 5½ by 8½ inches (14 by 21.5 cm).

This colorful case contains all the necessities for a good bridge game—except the friends and the food. **Design: Daphne Piester**

SUPPLIES

- Fabric, for the outer case and lining: ⅜ yard (.35 m)
- Assorted smaller fabric pieces for pockets and flaps
- Hook and loop tape, ¾ inch (2 cm) wide, 8 inches (20 cm)
- Hook and loop tape buttons for pocket flaps
- Stiff, non-corrugated cardboard: two pieces 5½ by 8½ inches (14 by 21.5 cm), and one piece 1¼ by 8½ inches (3 by 21.5 cm)

CUTTING

1. For the case, cut one outer fabric and one lining, 15¾ inches (40 cm) wide and 9¾ inches (24.5 cm) high.

2. Cut a strip for the pockets, 25 inches (63.5 cm) wide and 4¾ inches (12 cm) high. It will be cut into sections later. Cut pocket flaps after pocket sizes are determined.

CONSTRUCTION

Seam allowance is ⅜ inch (1 cm) except as noted.

1. Fold the the case lining piece in half with the short ends together and crease to mark the center. Lay it right side up on a table. Chalk a line ¾ inch (2 cm) to each side of the center crease to indicate the spine of the case. Chalk a line 1⅛ inch (2.5 cm) from each side to mark the flaps. Mark a line across the piece 1 inch (2.5 cm) from the lower edge of the piece and another the same distance from the top. Hem one long edge of the pocket strip.

2. Use the photo as a guide, and place cards, scorepad, and tally pads on the lining section within the marked lines. Start with the lower pocket. The pencil pocket will be at the spine. Fit the pocket piece over the items, keeping the lower edge even with the lining lower seamline. Pin small pleats at the lower edge as necessary. Allow slight ease in the fitting, and chalk mark the sides of the pockets to guide your stitching. Place pins between the pocket sections and at the sides. Trim off excess at the ends. Stitch the pocket to the lining along the marked divisions and stitch in the seam allowance around the outer edges.

3. Fit the upper pocket the same way, but press under the sides and lower edge and topstitch in place.

4. Make a flap for each pocket, if desired. With the pockets filled, measure the length of the flap from the top of the pocket, over the top of the item inside, to a point approximately 1 inch (2.5 cm) below the pocket edge. You can add hem allowance and hem the edges of each piece. As an alternative, use a double thickness of fabric with seam allowances added at all edges, stitch the pieces with right sides together, leaving an opening, then turn and topstitch. Add a hook an loop tape button at the underside of the flap and to the pocket front.

5. Pin the lining and outer cover piece with right sides together across the upper edge and along the sides. Stitch. Press the seam allowances to the wrong sides along the lower edge. Stitch along the marked spine and flap lines on the lining side. Insert the cardboard sections into the stitched compartments, trimming them if necessary, and topstitch closed across the lower edge.

6. Stitch a hook and loop tape strip to each flap. With the cover lining side up, attach the tape to the lining side of the left flap, and to the outer cover side of the right flap.

Hook and loop tape seals the flaps at the outer edge of the case.

117

Bike Bag

Instructions are on page 111
Enlarge pattern pieces 115%

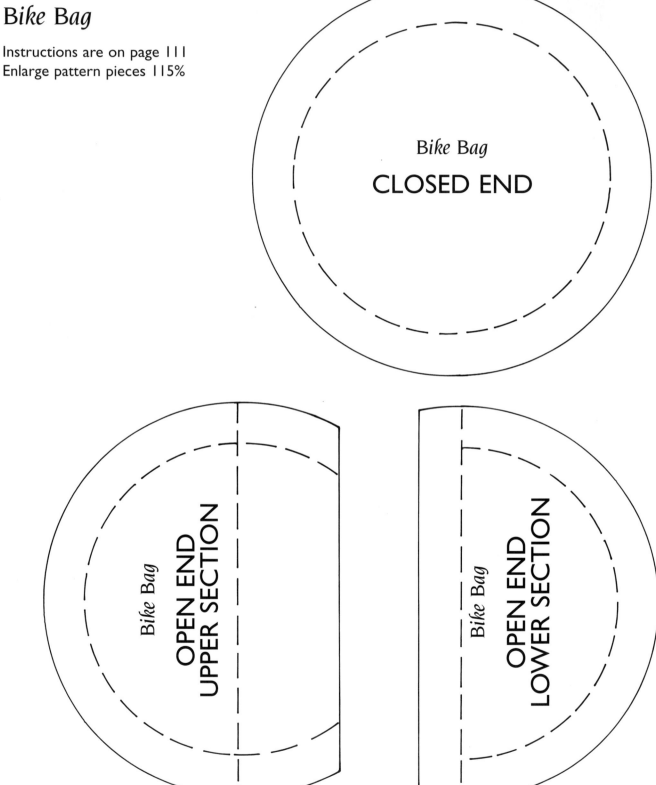

Bike Bag

CLOSED END

Bike Bag

**OPEN END
UPPER SECTION**

Bike Bag

**OPEN END
LOWER SECTION**

Especially for Kids

C hildren are happier travelers when they have their very own
luggage to pack and carry. Let them participate in the construction process too, helping with fabric selection, deciding about
pocket placement, and perhaps even stitching a seam or two.

Although we've designed these carryalls with children in
mind, the styles are perfectly appropriate for adults—and
every bit as useful. Once you have made the bag in the size
that's given, you will see that it is easy to enlarge it to a
grown-up's dimensions.

Child's Entertainment Pack

With this made-to-order, small-scale backpack, a child can choose, pack, *and* carry all the entertainment needed for a trip. Or a pre-filled pack can be given to the child at the beginning of the trip, loaded with surprises to make the miles seem shorter. The

bag's secret is the pockets—plenty of them! There are pockets for crayons, pencils, drawing paper, card games, a favorite stuffed toy, and anything else your little one requires. Much of the fun lies in exploring each pocket and finding unexpected treasure.

The model is made of pre-quilted fabric to eliminate the need for separate lining. Thin batting between the layers adds wearing comfort. The pack is 12 inches (31 cm) square and 2¼ inches (5.5 cm) deep, sized to fit a child approximately 3 to 7 years old.

SUPPLIES

- Pre-quilted fabric: 1 yard (1 m)
- Hook and loop tape: 9½-inch (24-cm) strip to close pack; additional for pocket closures if desired.
- Optional: elastic, ⅜ inch (1 cm) wide, for harness (see step 8)

CUTTING

The cutting and assembly instructions include an outer front pocket and a large one on the inner back, both of which are sewn into the side gusset seams. The rest are up to you! Smaller patch pockets can be added to the fronts of the two larger ones. Narrow pencil pockets can be sewn to the side gusset pieces. Several could be sewn to the inner front. For more about pockets, see page 7.

1. For the pack back/flap, cut a rectangle 13 by 19 inches (33 by 48 cm). For the front, cut a rectangle 13 by 14 inches (33 by 35.5 cm).

2. Cut one gusset strip, 39½ by 3 inches (100.5 by 7.5 cm). Cut two straps, 18 by 3¼ inches (46 by 8.5 cm). Note: check that straps will be long enough for the child who will wear the pack.

3. Cut the inner back pocket 13 by 11 inches (33 by 28 cm). Cut the outer front pocket 13 by 10 inches (33 by 25 cm). Cut additional pockets as desired.

CONSTRUCTION

Seam allowance is ⅜ inch (1 cm) except as noted.

1. If you will add smaller pockets to the outer front pocket or inner back pocket, do this first. Then add pockets to the inner front and/or side gussets.

2. Make the straps. Fold each strap section in half lengthwise, right sides together, and stitch along the long edge. Trim, turn, and press. Topstitch the long edges and clean finish the ends. Mark the center of the back/flap piece 6 inches (15.5 cm) below the flap edge. Fold under approximately 1½ inches (4 cm) at the upper end of each strap. Position one fold at either side of the center mark. Stitch approximately 1 inch (2.5 cm) of each end to the pack, stitching a square with an X within it for reinforcement. Fold the lower ends and position them at the lower corners of the back, the fold and the strap outer edge ¾ inch (2 cm) from the edge of the fabric. Stitch as for the upper ends.

3. Hem the upper (short) edge of the front and back pocket pieces. Place the front pocket on the pack front, both pieces right side up, sides and lower edges aligned. Baste together in the seam allowance. Position the back pocket, right side up, on the wrong side of the back/flap piece, sides and lower edges aligned. Baste.

4. Mark the seamline intersections at the lower corners of the back and front pieces. With right sides together, pin the gusset strip to the pack front. Clip the gusset seam allowance to fit it around each lower corner. Stitch.

5. Pin the back/flap piece to the other gusset edge in the same way, but begin and end the seam 1 inch (2.5 cm) below the upper ends of the gusset.

6. Fold under the upper edge of the front and side 1 inch (2.5 cm). Press, and zigzag along the hem edge. On the edges of the flap, fold the seam allowance to the inside and stitch the same way. Fold under 1 inch (2.5 cm) at the flap end and zigzag.

7. Sew one hook and loop tape section to the underside of the flap, close to the edge. Sew the remaining section to the pack front. approximately over the hemline stitching.

8. To keep the child's favorite stuffed toy secure in its back pocket, add an elastic "seatbelt." Cut two lengths of elastic, loop them once around each other, and stitch the ends inside the back pocket so that the strips form an X.

The pack does not include a side opening as shown on this model. We opened it this way to give you an idea of the pocket styles and shapes that can be added to the inside of the pack. **Design: Sarah Douglas**

Stuff Sack

Agood idea for every "kid" in the family, this is one of the handiest carryalls available for transporting or storing just about anything. It has enormous capacity, it is easy to open and close, and there is no hardware to malfunction or become detached. The bag is quick to assemble, and it lends itself to any sort of embellishment. Best, it can be made of almost any fabric and still work well and look fantastic.

The model in the photos is made of lightweight, waterproof nylon backpack fabric that is attractive and nearly indestructible. A decorative panel is fun to add: this one includes patchwork, satin stitched appliqué, and free-motion stitching with embroidery thread—and the designer's signature. You might adorn the bag with the owner's monogram, the school logo, or even add a photo transfer of the family pet.

For the beach, an overnight trip, or everyday needs, a stuff sack is always useful. **Design: Margaret Gregg**

SUPPLIES

- Fabric: 1¼ yards (1.15 m), 45 inches (115 cm) wide
- Lightweight batting: ⅜ yard (.35 m)
- Fabric scraps for appliqué and/or decorative thread for embellishment

CUTTING

1. For the carryall body, cut one piece, 21½ by 36½ inches (54.5 by 91.5 cm).

2. For the bag bottom, cut two circles from bag fabric and one from batting, 12 inches (30.5 cm) in diameter.

3. Cut one strap, 3½ by 77 inches (9 by 195.5 cm), piecing at the center if necessary. Cut one strap casing, 3½ by 37½ inches (9 by 95 cm).

4. Cut a bias strip 1¾ inches by 38 inches (4.5 by 97 cm).

5. Cut fabrics for appliqué or other decoration.

CONSTRUCTION

Seam allowance is ½ inch (1.5 cm) except as noted.

1. Apply decorations to the bag front—the center of the large panel.

2. Fold the carryall body section with the short ends right sides together. Stitch, then overcast or press under the seam allowances and topstitch.

3. Fold the strap in half lengthwise. Stitch the long edge and press the seam allowances to one side. Turn right side out. Center the seam, and topstitch through all layers.

4. Layer the fabric circles, right sides out with the batting between. Pin. Quilt the layers together with the stitching pattern you like best. Even the outer edge and stay stitch in the seam allowance. Trim the seam allowance to ¼ inch (.7 cm).

5. Attach the strap casing. Press the seam allowances to the wrong side at the ends of the strip. Stitch them in place. Beginning at the bag seam, pin the casing right side to the bag wrong side. Stitch. Press the seam open, and press under the seam allowance on the remaining long edge of the casing. Fold the casing to the bag right side along the seamline. Stitch the casing in place, stitching approximately ⅛ inch (3 mm) from the fold, and topstitch the upper edge.

6. Insert the strap through the casing. Pin the strap ends to the bottom of the bag, one on each side of the seam, the ends even with the bag lower edge. Stitch securely in the seam allowance. Pin the bias strip around the bottom, right sides together, folding under the end. Stitch and press. Fold the strip up over the seam allowance to just cover the previous stitching. Press, and stitch close to the fold.

The straps continue through a casing at the upper edge to close the top of the bag. Quilted layers at the bottom of the bag are a nice decorative feature and add to the bag's durability.

Let the child choose the fabric for an oversized duffel that performs equally well for travel or at-home storage. Window cases, made from fabric scraps, keep small items organized inside. **Design: Lori Kerr**

Quilted Duffel

A spacious duffel can serve many purposes. Filled with toys for a trip, it is a great traveler. It's a good bag for an overnight visit to a friend's house. And at home, it is a good place to store belongings.

The bag is made of medium-weight cotton, quilted to thick batting. It is lined with bright fabric and equipped with sturdy cotton webbing handles. The finished bag is approximately 30 inches (76 cm) wide, 16 inches (40.5 cm) high, and 6½ inches (16.5 cm) deep at the base. It is a simple matter to alter the size, and a good bag to make in many sizes.

SUPPLIES

- Outer bag fabric: 1¼ yards (1.15 m)
- Lining: 1¼ yards (1.15 m)
- Batting: one piece, 33 by 39 inches (84 by 99 cm)
- Webbing, for straps: 2½ yards (2.3 m), 1 inch (2.5 cm) wide
- Sport zipper, 20 inches (50.5 cm) long

CUTTING

1. Cut a rectangle from outer fabric and from lining, 33 by 39 inches (84 by 99 cm).

2. From outer fabric and from lining, cut two strips, 22 by 4¼ inches (56 by 11 cm).

CONSTRUCTION

Seam allowance is ⅝ (1.5 cm) inch except as noted.

1. Baste the batting to the wrong side of the outer fabric around the outer edges. Quilt the pieces, using free-motion stitching or the pattern of your choice. Trim the piece to square the edges. Place this piece on the lining and trim the lining to size.

2. Attach the handles. Lay the quilted piece right side up. Bring the ends of the webbing together to make a loop, and place it on the fabric so that the loop ends extend beyond the 33-inch (84-cm) sides and the webbing strips divide the piece approximately into thirds. Pin in place, stopping 2 inches (5 cm) from the fabric edges. The loops should measure approximately 18 inches (46 cm) between the pinned areas. Edgestitch the webbing in place. At the ends of the stitching, sew a square or X for reinforcement.

3. Fold the piece in half perpendicular to the webbing. Pin and stitch the sides. Press. Box the lower corners: Fold and crease the bottom between the side seams. With the bag wrong side out, arrange each lower corner to form a point as shown in the drawing on page 12, the side seam aligned with the pressed crease. Stitch across, stitching approximately 3 inches (7.5 cm) above the point and keeping the stitching line perpendicular to the seam and crease.

4. Make the zipper gusset. Fold each long bag fabric strip in half lengthwise, right side out. Press. Pin a strip to each side of the zipper, the fold on the zipper tape stitching line. Stitch close to the fold, and again near the edge of the zipper tape.

5. From bag fabric and from lining, cut two fabric strips 7 inches (18 cm) long and the width of the completed zipper gusset. Fold each bag fabric piece in half across, right side out, and place one over each end of the zipper, the folds near the ends of the teeth. Edgestitch to the zipper tape and across the ends of the zipper, avoiding the teeth. Fold the piece in half, lengthwise, to mark the center at each end. The lining pieces will be added later.

6. Install the zipper gusset. Open the zipper and pin the gusset to the bag opening with right sides together, the bag side seams at the marked points on the ends of the zipper gusset. It is easiest to stitch this with the zipper strip upward.

7. Fold the small lining pieces over the zipper ends on the bag inside. Baste at the sides, but don't stitch across the zipper. Stitch the lining side seams, leaving an opening on one side for turning. Box the lower corners.

To stitch the opening, reach through the opening at one of the zipper ends on the lining side.

8. Open the zipper. With right sides together, pin the lining and bag together along the zipper gusset edges, pinning the bag lining to the small lining sections at the ends of the gusset. Stitch. Turn right side out through the lining opening.

Window Cases

These are the simplest little bags imaginable to put together. They are a great way to help a child get organized.

The bag can be made any size. It is easiest to start with the zipper, then cut the fabric an inch or so wider than the zipper length and twice the desired length of the bag.

SUPPLIES

- Fabric rectangle
- Zipper
- Vinyl rectangle, for window
- Grosgrain ribbon, enough to surround the vinyl

CONSTRUCTION

1. Stitch the vinyl to the fabric wrong side with a narrow zigzag stitch, overcasting the edge at the same time. On the outside, cut away the fabric from in front of the vinyl, cutting close to the stitching.

2. Place the ribbon on the right side to cover the fabric raw edge around the window. Stitch along both edges of the ribbon.

3. Fold the fabric with right sides together, matching the short ends. Stitch ¾ inch (2 cm) or so at each end and baste the remainder of the seam. Install the zipper in the basted seam.

4. With the piece wrong side out, fold the tube to determine placement of the zipper on the bag. On the model shown, the zipper is approximately 1 inch (2.5 cm) below the fold at the top of the bag. Open the zipper and stitch the sides.

The Designers

Our sincere thanks to the designers who conjured up and created the wonderful bags and carriers shown on these pages. While many of these talented women are professional designers and fiber artists, many are women who, like us, sew for relaxation and personal pleasure whenever their busy schedules permit.

Dawn Anderson, Redmond, Washington, has designed and written for a number of craft books and magazines, inspired by the view of Mt. Ranier through her studio window.

dj Bennett, Lake Forest, Illinois, is known for her machine embroidery and fabric reconstruction skills. Her classes are popular throughout the U.S. and Canada, and she is the author of *The Machine Embroiderer's Handbook* (Lark Books, 1997), and of *Machine Embroidery with Style* (Madrona, 1980).

Pam Cauble, Asheville, North Carolina, is a hatmaker, Spanish teacher, and quilting enthusiast. She likes sewing fabrics almost as much as collecting them.

Sarah Douglas, Orinda, California, is adapt at many forms of hand needlework and an absolute magician at smocking. She is the author of *The Pleater Manual* (The Heirloom Collection, 1986).

Tracy Doyle, Herndon, Virginia, is a professional pattern maker and dressmaker. She teaches sewing and pattern making classes, and is author of *Patterns from Finished Clothes* (Sterling, 1996).

Lois Ericson, Salem, Oregon, is known for her imaginative fabric reconstruction techniques and clothing designs, and for her considerable teaching skills. She produces the *Design & Sew* garment pattern line, and is author of *Opening & Closing*, *What Goes Around*, *Design & Sew It Yourself* (with Linda Wakefield), and *Fabrics...Reconstructed*.

Margaret Gregg, Limestone, Tennessee, paints and sculpts in addition to working with all sorts of fiber techniques. Her studio, in an historic grist mill, supplies much of her inspiration.

Grace Grinnell, Bend, Oregon, retired at an early age from a corporate career to pursue her lifelong interest in designing expressive one-of-a-kind garments and accessories. She creates her own distinctive patterns, and enjoys working with unusual materials and findings.

Elma Johnson taught ceramics and fiber at the University of North Carolina-Asheville. Her successful designs encompass every imaginable medium, from bricks and glass to fabrics and fibers of all kinds.

Lori Kerr, Durham, North Carolina, is a professional designer who specializes in jewelry and textile art pieces, but experiments with just about anything that can be made of fabric. She enjoys sharing her skills through classes and workshops.

Kate Mathews, Barnardsville, North Carolina, is a freelance writer and editor of books about textile crafts. In the rare moments she is able to escape from the computer, she enjoys designing and making garments and accessories—especially with exotic fabrics.

Amy Mozingo, Asheville, North Carolina, operates a dressmaking and costume design business, putting to use the special fabrics she collects in her travels around the world. One of her recreational pleasures is crocheting with unusual yarns.

Tracy Munn, Asheville, North Carolina, has recently renovated an old barn to house a growing dressmaking and reupholstery business. In her "spare" time, she also enjoys stenciling and chair-seat weaving.

Mary Parker, Asheville, North Carolina, is a public sector finance officer who sews and teaches fabric techniques as creative recreation. She shares her studio space with an indulgent husband, a growing family of cats and, of course, an extensive fabric stash.

Nell Paulk, Atlanta, Georgia, likes to experiment with just about all of the needle arts. She is partial to out-of-the-ordinary materials and exceptional color schemes.

Daphne Piester, Brookneal, Virginia, is an ardent creator of almost anything that involves fabrics. She shares studio space with her husband Charles, an award-winning bird carver, and Pixie the cat.

Sheri Rand, Eugene, Oregon, teaches creative sewing and works at the design and repair of outdoor gear. She experiments continually, concentrating at the moment on silk painting and colorwash quilts.

Judith Robertson, Asheville, North Carolina, is the rare woman who actually sews up most of the fabric she acquires. In addition to making garments for herself and her family, she has a knack for creating useful accessories.

Pat Scheible, Mebane, North Carolina, works throughout the Southeast as a decorative painter. In her travels she has amassed the impressive collection of raw materials—primarily fabrics—that inspire her garment and project designs.

Julie Sibley, Young Harris, Georgia, is a rug designer and painter. She especially enjoys fabric painting and batik, and enjoys sharing her skills through classes and workshops.

Liz Spear, Waynesville, North Carolina, produces a line of distinctive custom garments and accessories made of her own handwoven fabrics. As a weaver, she respects even the smallest pieces of fabric, and finds innovative uses for them all.

Dee Dee Triplett, Bryson City, North Carolina, considers doll-making her primary focus. Travels around the country to teach her craft provide her the opportunity to collect still more fabric. She enjoys the challenge of creating useful articles—as long as they are visually appealing as well.

Acknowledgements

We would like to express our appreciation to the following people and businesses who contributed to this book in one or another essential way by loaning us props, modeling for a photo or two, or providing a photogenic location at which to take the pictures.

Warren Fluharty Designs
J.M. Hearn & Company
Henco Drafting & Art Supplies
The Loft
The Natural Home

The Old Depot Association, Black Mountain, NC
Tressa's Downtown Jazz and Blues Club
Our models: Lucy Ballentine, Evans Carter, and Catharine Sutherland

Index

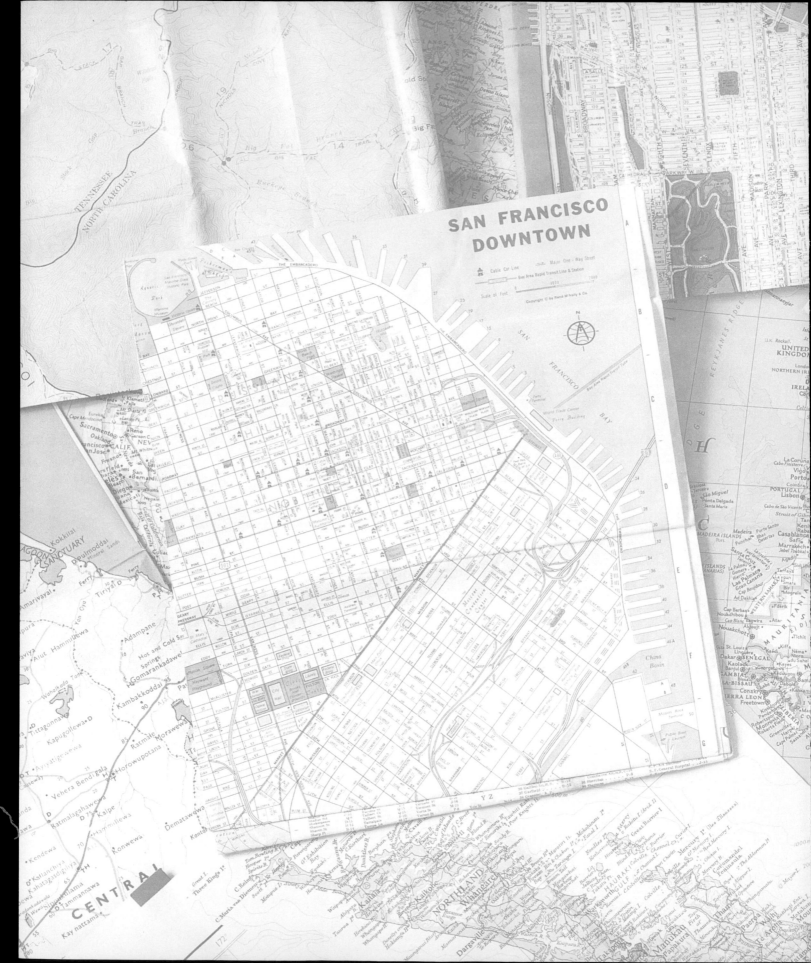